25

BICYCLE TOURS
in and around
Washington, D.C.

25
BICYCLE TOURS
in and around
Washington, D.C.

From the Capitol Steps to Country Roads

Anne H. Oman
Photographs by Anne H. Oman and Tabitha R. Oman

SECOND EDITION

Backcountry Publications
Woodstock · Vermont

An Invitation to the Reader

Although it is unlikely that the roads you cycle on these tours will change much with time, some road signs, landmarks, and other terms may. If you find that changes have occurred on these routes, please let us know so we may correct them in future editions. Address all correspondence to:

Editor
25 Bicycle Tours© Series
Backcountry Publications
PO Box 748
Woodstock, VT 05091

Library of Congress Cataloging-in-Publication Data

Oman, Anne H.

25 bicycle tours in and around Washington, D.C.: from the capitol steps to country roads / Anne H. Oman ; photographs by Anne H. Oman and Tabitha R. Oman. —2nd ed.

    p. cm. — (25 bicycle tours book)

  ISBN 0-88150-422-X (alk. paper)

  1. Bicycle touring—Washington Region—Guidebooks. 2. Bicycle trails—Washington Region—Guidebooks. 3. Washington (D.C.)—Guidebooks. I. Title. II. Series.

GV 1045.5.W2053 1999
917.5304'41—dc21   98-13692
                                                      CIP

Published by Backcountry Publications, a division of
The Countryman Press, PO Box 748, Woodstock, VT 05091

Distributed by W. W. Norton & Company, Inc.,
500 Fifth Avenue, New York, NY 10110

Text and cover design by Sally Sherman
Cover photograph by Anne H. Oman
Maps by XNR Productions, © 1998 The Countryman Press
Photographs by Anne H. Oman and Tabitha R. Oman

Printed in the United States of America
10 9 8 7 6 5 4 3 2 1

Acknowledgments

I'd like to thank all of the people who went on these tours with me, especially my family, the Gourleys, the Martins, Tato Joelson, Dwayne Poston, Erik Smith, Joslin Frank, Lynn Newbury, Hubert Shaiyen, Christian Buhl, and Betsy Agle. They endured rain, wrong turns, and other tribulations in the interest of research for this book. I would also like to thank Carl Taylor, who inspired and encouraged me to undertake this project.

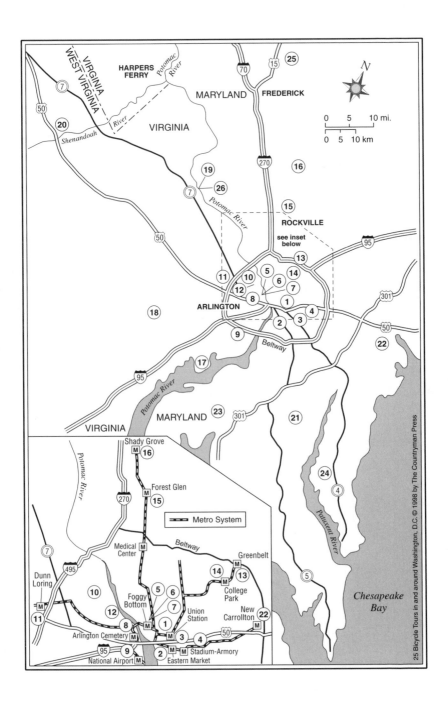

Contents

Introduction

Washington is a big, booming metropolis, but a great place to bike. A system of trails, a disproportionate number of national and local parks, a subway system accessible to cyclists at certain times, and a network of activist cyclists who lobby for better bicycling conditions all combine to make the Washington area hospitable to two-wheeled touring. The Washington area also has an amazing variety of natural and built attractions—from the Great Falls of the Potomac to the Washington Cathedral, from the shore of the Chesapeake Bay to the Civil War town of Harpers Ferry. Seeing these places by bicycle gives them added interest.

About the Rides

The tours in this book are designed to take the rider to well-known and lesser-known places within the city of Washington and its suburbs—and to facilitate getaways to rural areas surprisingly close to the city. The rides will appeal most to people who like to combine cycling with visiting historic and scenic points of interest.

There are rides in this book to suit just about every level of cycling ability and every time frame. A short ride around the National Arboretum or through Arlington Cemetery makes a nice family activity on a Sunday afternoon. The trip to Harpers Ferry is ideal for a weekend, and the trip to Waterford and Middleburg could be stretched to three days or completed in two. Most of the trips can easily be completed in one day—but some can be stretched into overnight trips if schedules permit. The people who made the trips with me ranged in age from 7 to 50-plus. You can set your own pace on these tours. If you have children or people unused to cycling in your party, you'll want to take more rest stops and allow extra time to walk up some hills.

Because different cyclists set different paces, I haven't tried to estimate the time necessary to complete a tour. You can spend all day on a 10-mile tour if you stop often to rest, picnic, swim, and see the sights. On the other hand, you can easily ride 40 to 50 miles in less than a day.

I found 25 miles to be a good distance for a one-day tour—challenging enough but allowing time for poking around old cemeteries or wading in streams. I've tried to avoid backtracking, but sometimes this wasn't possible.

About the Metro

Many of the tours start from Metrorail stations. Bicyclists are allowed to bring their bikes on the trains weekdays between 10 AM and 2 PM and after 7 PM and at any time on weekends and most federal holidays. Permits are no longer required. Bicyclists must use the last car on the train and enter it through either the first or last doors, not the middle door. The number of bikes per train is limited. Using the Metro is great because it gets you nearer to your destination, without the bother and expense of car bike racks. Call 202-962-1116 for more information and to make sure the no-permit policy is still operative. If you don't want to use Metrorail, many of the stations have parking lots that are free on weekends. For more information about parking at Metro stations, call 202-637-7000.

About Safety

Cycling in a metropolitan area involves two kinds of safety considerations. A cyclist needs to protect himself or herself from criminal activity as well as from traffic hazards. The tours in this book are all in areas considered safe, in daylight hours, at the time of publication. But "safe" is a relative term, and no place is completely without danger. Prudent cyclists will use common sense to protect themselves and their bikes against crime and other dangers. Here are some important safety tips:

- Never ride alone, particularly on a secluded trail or road.
- Always let someone know what route you are taking.
- Don't ride after dark.
- Carry a whistle around your neck or an air horn in an accessible pocket. Noise can both bring help and scare away attackers.
- Ride with the traffic flow. This is a legal requirement.
- Wear a helmet. (See "About Equipment.")
- Use hand signals before turning. A left arm out straight signals a left turn. A left arm bent upward at a right angle signals a right turn. A left arm bent downward at a right angle signals slowing or stopping.
- When riding with companions, ride single file at least 20 feet apart.

The U.S. Capitol sits atop 120 acres of groomed grounds landscaped by Frederick Law Olmsted, the architect of New York City's Central Park.

- Don't wear headsets or ear plugs.
- Be sure your bicycle is in good working order.
- Watch out for storm drains, potholes, railroad or trolley tracks, patches of sand or gravel, and other road hazards.
- Ride defensively. Cars are bigger than you are. Watch for people opening the doors of parked cars on your side of the road.
- Pull well away from the road when you stop to rest or check the map.

Bike Security

Always secure your bike when you leave it—even for a few minutes. This is especially important in urban areas, where bicycle theft is a serious problem. The kind of lock most likely to foil would-be bicycle thieves is the U-shaped shackle lock, sold under such brand names as Kryptonite and Citadel. These are expensive—but not as expensive as a new bicycle. And police departments in some jurisdictions report that bicycle thefts have actually declined since these locks were introduced in the 1970s. Here are some basic security guidelines:

- Lock your bike to something permanent and in a place where any attempted theft is likely to be noticed.
- Lock up as much of your bike as possible. If you have quick-release wheels, remove the front wheel and put the lock through the front wheel, the rear wheel, and the frame, securing it to the rack, tree, or other fixture. Remove any accessories you don't want to lose— pumps, water bottles, and computer-type odometers are vulnerable to theft.
- Register your bike with your local police department. This will greatly enhance your chances of getting it back if it's stolen.

About Equipment

All you really need are a touring or mountain bike in good condition, a helmet, a lock (see above), and clothing suitable for the weather. The Washington Area Bicyclist Association (WABA) publishes a *Consumer's Guide to Bicycle Helmets*. To obtain a copy, call 202-628-2500.

Other useful equipment includes a patch kit and spare tube, a bike-mounted air pump, a bike-mounted water bottle, a rear-view mirror attached either to your helmet or to your handlebars, an odometer (either the computer type that is installed on your handlebars or the less expensive mechanical variety that attaches on your front wheel), and some kind of carrying device. Packs that attach to your bike are more comfortable than backpacks.

Bike Rentals

Many bicycle shops rent bikes, racks, child carriers, helmets, and other equipment. If you want to rent a bike for a particular tour, call the bike shop listed at the end of the tour. In addition, rental bikes are available at Fletcher's Boat House (202-244-0461) on the Chesapeake and Ohio Canal and at Thompson Boat Center (202-333-4861), convenient to the C&O Canal Trail, the Rock Creek Trail, and D.C. monuments.

Sources for Maps and Other Information

Maps in this book are designed to provide all the information bicyclists taking these tours will need. However, you can obtain additional maps and tips from the various political jurisdictions—states, counties, etc. An easier method is to send a self-addressed, stamped envelope to the Washington Area Bicyclist Association (WABA) and ask for a list of maps and other guides. WABA will send you an order form and will fill your request promptly. You may also visit the association's shop to purchase your maps: 1511 K Street NW, Suite 1015, Washington, D.C. 20005 (202-628-2500).

Organized Cycling

Several organizations in the Washington area run frequent group cycling trips. Foremost among these are:

Potomac Pedalers Touring Club. Each weekend, the Potomac Pedalers run a dozen or more trips for cyclists of varying abilities. The group rates each ride according to seven categories, which range from "Casual" (from 5 to 15 miles in length), to "Fast Training" (for race-oriented cyclists). Nonmembers are welcome on the rides, but it's difficult to find out about them if you're not a member. The schedule is published in the club newsletter, *Pedal Patter,* which is mailed to members and is also available at some bicycle shops. Each ride has a leader, whose phone number is listed in the newsletter description in case a reader needs more information. There are no charges for the rides. For membership information, call 202-363-TOUR.

American Youth Hostels. This group offers rides most weekends, usually recreational rides to points of interest and suitable for casual cyclists. Most rides include a lunch or snack stop, and the ride fee covers this plus van transportation from the Washington hostel at 11th and K Streets NW. For a recorded message about currently scheduled tours, call 202-783-4944. The recording includes a number to call for further information.

Bike the Sites, Inc. offers professionally guided bike tours to various tourist attractions, including Mount Vernon. The fee includes a bicycle and helmet. Call 202-966-8662 for more information.

In addition, other groups offer rides on an occasional basis. Check for "Cycling" in the sports listings in Friday's "Weekend" section of the *Washington Post.*

CITY AND SUBURBS

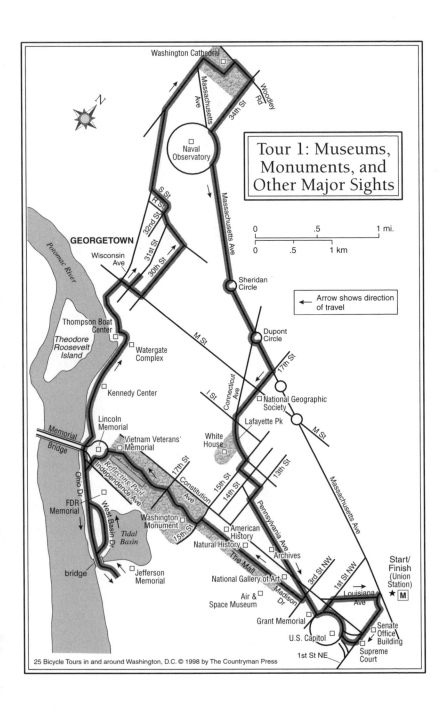

Washington Cathedral

Massachusetts Ave

34th St

Woodley Rd

Naval Observatory

Tour 1: Museums, Monuments, and Other Major Sights

S St

R St

32nd St

GEORGETOWN

Wisconsin Ave

31st St

30th St

Potomac River

Sheridan Circle

Massachusetts Ave

0   .5   1 mi.

0   .5   1 km

← Arrow shows direction of travel

M St

Dupont Circle

Thompson Boat Center

17th St

Theodore Roosevelt Island

Watergate Complex

Connecticut Ave

I St

National Geographic Society

M St

Kennedy Center

Lafayette Pk

Lincoln Memorial

White House

13th St

Memorial Bridge

Vietnam Veterans' Memorial

Reflecting Pool

17th St

15th St

14th St

Constitution Ave

Ohio Dr

Independence Ave

Pennsylvania Ave

Massachusetts Ave

FDR Memorial

West Basin Dr

Washington Monument

15th St

American History

Natural History

Archives

Tidal Basin

The Mall

3rd St NW

1st St NW

Start/ Finish (Union Station)

★ M

bridge

Jefferson Memorial

National Gallery of Art

Madison Dr

Louisiana Ave

Air & Space Museum

Grant Memorial

U.S. Capitol

Senate Office Building

Supreme Court

1st St NE

1
Museums, Monuments, and Other Major Sights

Location: *District of Columbia*
Metro access: *Union Station*
Terrain: *One fairly steep uphill climb, otherwise flat with only a few moderate hills*
Road conditions: *Bike paths and some city streets with light traffic on weekends*
Distance: *10.6 miles*
Highlights: *Washington's major monuments and museums plus Georgetown, Embassy Row, the White House*

This is a great tour if you're a newcomer to Washington or if you want to show visitors your city from a different perspective. (To find out where you can rent bikes for visitors, see the list of bicycle shops at the end of this chapter.) While it will only take a couple of hours to breeze by all these attractions, you can easily spend all day on this tour if you actually visit the sights. Be sure to bring good bike locks.

Start your tour at Union Station, either at the Metro stop or in the pay parking lot. Be sure to take time either before or after the tour to explore the station building, which is loosely modeled on Rome's Baths of Caracalla. Still in use as a major train station, it also holds shops, restaurants, food stands, and nine movie theaters.

> *0.0 Cross Massachusetts Avenue in the pedestrian crosswalk in front of the Christopher Columbus fountain. Turn left; then take a right onto First Street NE. Ride up the hill, between the Russell and Dirksen Senate Office Buildings and past the Supreme Court.*

0.5 Turn right onto the grounds of the U.S. Capitol.

Park your bike in the rack on the north side of the building and enter by climbing the steps in the center of the east side. You'll then be in the Rotunda, under the cast-iron dome, where tours run all day, every day, between 9 AM and 4:30 PM. After the tour, walk out on the West Terrace for a view of the Mall and the Washington Monument and Lincoln Memorial.

Reclaim your bike and head down Capitol Hill.

0.8 You may want to rest here and admire the Grotto.

This sylvan structure was designed by Frederick Law Olmsted, who landscaped the Capitol grounds as well as New York's Central Park. The small brick shelter was built around a spring, but the spring turned impure and was replaced by a water fountain.

At the bottom of the hill, cross First Street NW, circling around the Navy Memorial.

0.9 Stop at the Grant Memorial, one of the capital's most compelling, and bike around the north rim of the Capitol Reflecting Pool. Cross Third Street NW and enter Madison Drive, which parallels the Mall on the north side.

1.3 The National Gallery of Art is on your right.

It includes the angular I.M. Pei East Wing—which houses Calder mobiles, Joan Miró tapestries, and changing exhibits—and the classical West Wing, home to paintings ranging from the Renaissance to the 20th century. There's a bike rack at the east entrance to the West Wing.

Continue along Madison Drive, stopping to visit museums and other attractions at will.

1.4 The National Air and Space Museum is on the left across the Mall.

The National Archives, repository of the Constitution and the Declaration of Independence, is on your right across Constitution Avenue.

1.5 The National Museum of Natural History is on your right.

It houses the Hope diamond, an insect zoo, dinosaur skeletons, and millions of other artifacts. Across the Mall is the Smithsonian

Kite flyers lend a festive air to the 555-foot obelisk memorializing George Washington. The monument's cornerstone was laid in 1848 with the same trowel Washington had used to set the cornerstone of the Capitol.

"Castle," which holds the tomb of James Smithson. The scholarly, illegitimate son of an English lord, Smithson left his fortune to establish in the United States an institution devoted to knowledge, even though he never visited this country. Adjacent to the castle is a carousel.

1.6 Across the Mall is a complex of underground museums devoted to Asian, African, and Pacific Island art.

Adjacent to this complex is the aboveground Freer Gallery, with a fine collection of Asian art plus representative paintings by Winslow Homer, James Whistler, and others. A highlight is the "Peacock" dining room designed and decorated by Whistler.

1.7 Park your bike in the rack in front of the National Museum of American History and browse through the eclectic collection.

It includes the inaugural ball gowns of all the first ladies, the red slippers from the movie *The Wizard of Oz,* and the original flag that inspired Francis Scott Key to write "The Star-Spangled Banner." The Mall ends here, at 14th Street, but Madison Drive continues one more block to 15th Street.

1.9 Cross 15th Street in the pedestrian crossing and ride up the hill to the Washington Monument.

Even if you don't want to wait in line long enough to ascend, you'll have a fine view of the Lincoln Memorial and the Reflecting Pool ahead of you and of the White House to your right.

Take the path that veers off to your right and follow it to the crosswalk across 17th Street.

2.2 Walk your bike across 17th Street in the crosswalk and enter the wide, hard-packed dirt trail that runs beside the Reflecting Pool.

The pool was modeled on those leading to the palace at Versailles and to the Taj Mahal.

2.5 Lock your bike in the rack near the information kiosk and visit the Lincoln Memorial, the Korean War Memorial, and the Vietnam Veterans Memorial.

There are rest rooms under the Lincoln Memorial. If you visit them, you can also view the stalactites growing under the monument.

Follow the sidewalk to your left around the memorial and cross Independence Avenue near the Ericson Memorial, dedicated to the inventor of the screw propeller. Cross Ohio Drive and enter the bike path, heading left.

You may want to rest under the willows on the banks of the Potomac and gaze over at Arlington House, home of Robert E. Lee, on the Virginia side.

2.9 *Turn left into the Franklin Delano Roosevelt Memorial, which opened in 1997.*

Built of red South Dakota granite and resplendent with waterfalls and realistic bronze sculpture, the memorial was designed by Lawrence Halprin. FDR in a flowing cape with his dog Fala by his side is one of the most popular attractions. The Depression figures—including an urban breadline, a rural couple, and a man pressed to an old-fashioned radio listening to a "fireside chat"— are by noted sculptor George Segal.

3.3 *Exit the last of the outdoor "rooms" that make up the FDR Memorial and follow the paved path across the grass toward the bridge. Cross the bridge over the Tidal Basin.*

Observe the fish-tailed gargoyles on the bridge. They were added in 1987 and their faces were copied from a photograph of the then head of the National Park Service, Jack Fish.

As soon as you've crossed the bridge, bear left to the Jefferson Memorial. After visiting the memorial, double back across the bridge and take West Basin Drive to your right.

This will lead you past the famous cherry trees, a gift from Japan.

3.9 *At the fork, bear left, following the signs toward the Lincoln Memorial. Cross Ohio Drive and reenter the bike path, heading right.*

4.2 *Pass under Memorial Bridge, where the path narrows. Walk your bike.*

4.3 *The Watergate Steps, which preceded the famous apartment complex by several decades, served as a ceremonial entry to Washington for VIPs arriving by sea.*

Later, but before airplane and road noise precluded the idea, the steps were the site of concerts. Old-movie buffs may remember that Sophia Loren skipped out of a concert here to begin her romance with Cary Grant in *Houseboat.*

4.9 *On your right is the Kennedy Center for the Performing Arts and, just beyond it, the Watergate Complex.*

5.1 *Turn left to the Thompson Boat Center (bike and boat rentals available); then bear right and walk your bike on the brick sidewalk that leads along the newly renovated Georgetown waterfront.*

You'll pass fountains, outdoor cafés, and a realistic sculpture of a man in a turtleneck and cap filling his pipe. Across the river (left) lies Theodore Roosevelt Island, a nature preserve. You'll probably see crews and individuals rowing on the river.

5.2 *Turn right, exit the waterfront complex, and enter Wisconsin Avenue, riding uphill.*

5.3 *Cross a bridge over the C&O Canal (see Tour 7). Continue up Wisconsin to M Street and turn right.*

Watch for heavy traffic in the heart of the Georgetown commercial area.

5.4 *Cross M Street at 31st in the pedestrian crosswalk and walk your bike to the Old Stone House at 3051 M Street NW.*

Built in 1765, the oldest surviving residential structure in the city is open for tours Wednesday through Sunday. It was the home of a cabinetmaker and his family and provides a rare glimpse of what life was like for the middle class in the 18th century. The garden in back is a great place for picnics, and carryout food is available at several places on M Street.

Continue east on M Street to 30th Street; then turn left up 30th Street through the fashionable 19th-century Georgetown residential district.

5.8 *Turn left onto R Street, skirting Oak Hill Cemetery and Montrose Park (right).*

At 31st and R Streets is the entrance to Dumbarton Oaks Gardens, containing formal and informal gardens and fountains and an "orangerie." The gardens are open 2–6 PM daily, and there is an admission charge.

5.9 Turn right onto 32nd Street.

The Dumbarton Oaks Museum, including the house where the representatives from major powers met to lay the foundation for the United Nations, the pre-Columbian collection, and the Byzantine collection, is located at 1703 32nd Street. It's open Tuesday through Sunday 2–5 PM, and a donation is suggested.

6.0 Turn left onto S Street, then right onto Wisconsin Avenue. Be prepared for heavy traffic and a steep climb.

6.7 On your left is the former Soviet Embassy's residential and office complex on a site known as Mount Alto.

Before glasnost, a great brouhaha developed when it was discovered that from this elevated site, the Soviets could intercept secret signals.

6.9 Turn right onto South Road on the Washington Cathedral grounds.

This Gothic cathedral, in the style of 14th-century English ecclesiastical architecture, was begun in 1907 and completed in 1990. Volunteers give tours and point out the moon rock incorporated into a stained-glass window, the crypt of Woodrow Wilson (the only president buried in the District of Columbia), and other features. An elevator takes visitors to the Pilgrim Gallery for a spectacular view from one of Washington's highest points.

After visiting the cathedral, take the road to the right of the building, past the peaceful Bishops Garden. Bear left at the nursery and exit the cathedral grounds at Woodley Road NW.

7.1 Turn right onto Woodley Road.

7.2 Turn right onto 34th Street. Watch for heavy traffic.

7.7 Turn left onto Massachusetts Avenue NW.

As soon as you make the turn, you'll see the U.S. Naval Observatory on your right. You may enter only if you go on one of the 90-minute tours, which are held weekdays at 12:30 and 2 PM. On the grounds is the vice president's house, which is not open to the public.

8.0 The British Embassy complex is on your right.

It includes a modern office building that was added onto the residence designed by Sir Edward Luytens, architect of many of the great country houses of England. In front of the residence, with one foot on the embassy's British soil and one foot on American soil, is a statue of Winston Churchill, cigar in hand.

8.1 The embassies of Bolivia and Brazil are on the right.

Across the avenue is the old Iranian Embassy, which was commandeered by the State Department during the hostage crisis.

8.2 The Islamic Center and Mosque is on your left.

It was built with monetary and material contributions from many Moslem countries. Note that it does not face the street exactly—it faces Mecca. Non-Moslem visitors are welcome. You must remove your shoes before entering.

8.3 The Embassy of Japan is on your right; the Embassy of Venezuela is on your left.

8.5 The United Arab Emirates Embassy is on your right.

The limestone château across the avenue, designed in 1906 by local architect George Oakley Totten, serves as the Embassy of Cameroon.

8.6 Yield to traffic in Sheridan Circle, which contains a statue of General Sheridan on his horse, Rienzi.

The work is nicknamed "an officer and a gentleman." On your right is the Embassy of Turkey.

8.7 Anderson House is on your right.

It contains a museum of artifacts of the Society of the Cincinnati, an organization of descendants of George Washington's officers, and a lovely garden. It's open for tours afternoons Tuesday through Saturday.

8.8 The Embassy of Indonesia is on your right.

The embassy occupies the former home of Evelyn Walsh McLean, whose father struck it rich in the Colorado goldfields and who owned the Hope diamond.

Continue on Massachusetts Avenue through Dupont Circle.

9.1 *Turn right onto 17th Street NW and continue to the intersection of 17th and M Streets.*

Lock your bike to a tree or sign and visit Explorers Hall of the National Geographic Society. It's open daily and the changing exhibits are free.

Continue south on 17th Street.

9.5 *At I Street, 17th Street intersects with Connecticut Avenue. Bear left onto Connecticut to Lafayette Park.*

The square surrounding the park is actually known as Jackson Square, and although there is a statue of Lafayette in the park, the central place is occupied by an equestrian statue of Andrew Jackson, his horse rearing in the direction of the house he once occupied. Washington's elite—including Henry Adams, John Hay, Dolley Madison, and Stephen Decatur—lived on this square. Many of the houses have been preserved and are used as government offices. The Stephen Decatur House, on the northwest corner of the square, is open to the public. You may also visit St. John's, "the church of Presidents," at the corner of 16th and H Streets.

Walk your bike through the park and cross Pennsylvania Avenue, now a pedestrian mall, in front of the White House.

The White House is open for tours mornings Tuesday through Saturday. Expect a long line.

Turn left and follow Pennsylvania Avenue past the Treasury Building.

9.7 *Following the inaugural parade route—but backward—turn right onto 15th Street NW. Just past the Treasury Building, cross in the pedestrian crossing into Pershing Square.*

The square contains a memorial to Gen. "Black Jack" Pershing plus an ice-skating rink that turns into a water garden in summer.

Cross 14th Street and enter the Western Plaza, with its fountains and inscriptions about the city.

On your right is the Beaux Arts–style District Building, Washington's city hall.

Walk or ride across the plaza; then cross Pennsylvania Avenue and continue riding down the "avenue of presidents."

9.9 *The Old Post Office Building, saved from the wrecking ball in the 1970s, holds shops and restaurants.*

There's a great view from the tower. Across Pennsylvania Avenue is the Hoover Building, FBI headquarters. The popular tours of this building are available weekdays 8:45 AM to 4:15 PM. Expect to wait in line.

10.0 *The Navy Memorial and bandstand (left) was undertaken as part of the Pennsylvania Avenue spruce-up.*

10.1 *Modern and monumental, the Canadian Embassy (left) is the first embassy to be built on Pennsylvania Avenue. Its gallery features works by Canadian artists and is open to the public.*

10.3 *Pennsylvania Avenue NW ends at the foot of Capitol Hill. Turn left onto First Street NW and follow it past the intersection with Constitution Avenue. Bear right onto Louisiana Avenue.*

10.6 *Return to the starting point, Union Station.*

Bicycle Repair Service

Big Wheel Bikes, 1034 33rd Street NW (202-337-0254)

The Bike Shop at District Hardware, 2003 P Street NW (202-659-8686)

2

Wandering Washington's Waterfront

Location: The district of Columbia
Metro access: Eastern Market
Terrain: Flat
Road conditions: Paved bike trails, park roads, and city streets
Distance: 16 miles
Highlights: Marinas, military installations, memorials, and markets
along Washington's waterfront

No one would characterize Washington as a port city, but it does have a historic and lively waterfront, and cycling provides a great way to tour it. This tour begins at the Eastern Market Metro stop on Capitol Hill, passes the Marine Barracks and the home of the Corps commandant, and pays a visit to the historic Washington Navy Yard, with its museums and a destroyer that visitors can board. The trip continues to a picturesque marina on the southwest waterfront, to the National War College and homes of the Army brass at Fort Lesley J. McNair, and to the part of the waterfront that was "concretized" during the urban renewal craze of the 1950s. After a stop at the pungent Maine Avenue Fish Market and a ride around Hains Point, the tour takes in the Tidal Basin and the Jefferson Memorial and returns to the starting point via the Mall and the Smithsonian Museums.

> *0.0 From the Eastern Market Metro stop, proceed to the corner of Pennsylvania Avenue and Eighth Street SE and turn right, heading south on Eighth Street.*

> *0.2 On your left, at the corner of G Street SE, is the home of the commandant of the U.S. Marine Corps.*

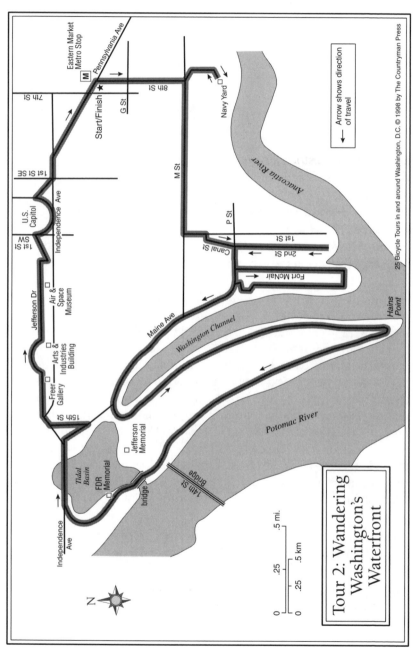

Tour 2: Wandering Washington's Waterfront

25 Bicycle Tours in and around Washington, D.C. © 1998 by The Countryman Press

The house dates from 1805 and is surrounded by the redbrick Marine Barracks and the parade grounds.

0.5 *Eighth Street ends. Cross M Street SE at the light. You'll be at the ceremonial gate to the Washington Navy Yard. As this entrance is used only by residents and VIPs, turn left onto M Street.*

0.7 *Turn right and enter the Navy Yard through the public gate. Follow the signs to the historic district, and you'll come to the old Commandant's Office.*

During the Civil War, this two-story frame building with wraparound porches also served as the home of Commandant John Dahlgren. Lincoln used to come here late at night to play cards. Just behind the Commandant's Office is the Navy Museum, which occupies one of the buildings of the gun factory that once made much of the ammunition and weapons used by the Navy. The museum charts the history of the U.S. Navy from the Revolution to the present, and exhibits include gun decks, a submarine room with working periscopes, and historical memorabilia. Admission is free, and the museum is open daily.

Across the parking lot, in a long, low, narrow building where the Navy once tested model ships, is a museum devoted to the history of submarines. In Willard Park, in front of the Navy Museum, is an outdoor display of military weapons and hardware, plus a few picnic tables. At the Anacostia River waterfront is the U.S.S. Barry, a destroyer commissioned in 1956 and now a permanent visit ship at the Navy Yard. The Barry, which saw action in waters off Cuba and Vietnam, is open daily for self-guided tours.

After your tour, backtrack to the gate.

1.6 *Turn left onto M Street SE. Watch for traffic. After crossing South Capitol Street, you'll be in the southwest quadrant of the District.*

2.7 *Turn left onto First Street SW.*

2.8 *Turn right onto Canal Street; at P Street, make a left onto Second Street. Continue down Second Street past the side of Fort McNair.*

3.7 On your right is the James Creek Marina.

This is a perfect place to rest and watch the boats bobbing in the water. There are picnic tables shaded by tall oaks, a soda machine, and ducks to feed. There's a great view of the National War College (across the water).

After your respite, double back on Second Street.

4.4 Turn left onto P Street.

Note the bayonet motif on the top of the redbrick wall surrounding Fort McNair.

4.6 Turn left and stop at the checkpoint at the main gate of Fort McNair.

You must show a picture ID to enter, and you must wear a helmet.

Bear right around the parade ground, then left in front of the gracious brick houses—homes of the Army's top generals—that back on the Washington Channel.

5.1 At the Officers' Club, turn right and then left, following the road that runs along the breakwater.

5.3 The road veers left and leads to the massive Beaux-Arts building designed by Stanford White that houses the National War College.

You may want to pause on a bench between the water and the golf course and drink in the view of Hains Point and of Alexandria in the distance across the Potomac.

After passing the War College, the road curves to the left and leads you along the other side of the parade ground, past the homes of noncommissioned officers.

6.4 Leave Fort McNair via the main gate and turn left. Follow the sidewalk, which leads into a pedestrian walkway between apartment buildings.

6.5 The Titanic Memorial (left) honors the men who gave up their places on the lifeboats and died in the Titanic disaster.

The granite figure, which represents self-sacrifice, was sculpted by Gertrude Vanderbilt Whitney.

6.5 The walkway turns right here, following the waterfront past

The white marble Jefferson Memorial echoes the style of the Rotunda at the University of Virginia, which was designed by Jefferson.

docks where the fireboats, marine police boats, and excursion vessels are moored and on past several large marinas.

Some of the restaurants that line the waterfront have seasonal outdoor-seating areas.

7.4 The walkway ends, but continue straight across the parking lot into the Maine Avenue Fish Market.

The fish are all trucked in now and sold from boats permanently moored here. Exit the fish market and continue in the same direction, past a marine store, on the sidewalk that leads under a bridge.

7.9 Follow the sidewalk around to the left and enter East Potomac Park.

Ride past the tennis bubble, swimming pool, and miniature golf course on the road alongside the Washington Channel. Fort McNair and the southwest waterfront restaurants now lie across the channel.

10.0 At the end of the road is Hains Point.

The point is marked by cedars and a sculpture known as the *Awakening,* which consists of a half-buried bronze figure. Playgrounds, picnic tables, rest rooms, and water are available here.

Follow the road back along the other side of the peninsula, along the Potomac River.

You'll see a lot of people fishing, and you'll get a good view of planes taking off from National Airport across the river.

12.0 After passing under the 14th Street Bridge, carry your bike up the set of steps to your right and cross the bridge over the Tidal Basin. Follow either the road or the walkway along the Tidal Basin, which is lined with cherry trees and filled with pedal boats.

The Jefferson Memorial, designed by John Russell Pope, is the centerpiece of the Tidal Basin. Along the west side of the basin stands the Franklin Delano Roosevelt Memorial, whose four outdoor "rooms" represent each of Roosevelt's terms as president.

12.6 At the fork, bear right, following the sign for Independence Avenue. At Independence Avenue, turn right and cross the

bridge over the Tidal Basin. When the road divides, bear right along the basin onto Maine Avenue, past the entrance to the pedal boat concession.

13.5 *Turn left onto 15th Street, crossing at the light, and climb a slight hill.*

You'll pass the Bureau of Printing and Engraving, where folding money is printed, and the Holocaust Museum, devoted to documentation and memorabilia of people murdered and persecuted by the Nazis.

13.7 *Cross Independence Avenue and turn right onto Jefferson Drive, which runs along the Mall.*

14.0 *The Freer Gallery (right) houses Oriental art and paintings by American artists.*

Of particular interest is the "Peacock" dining room, designed for a home in London by James Whistler. Adjacent to the Freer, behind the redbrick Smithsonian "castle," is a Victorian garden and the entrance to underground museums devoted to Far Eastern and African art.

14.3 *The Arts and Industries Building (right) contains artifacts from the nation's centennial exposition held in 1876 in Philadelphia.*

Next door is the Hirshhorn Gallery and (left) its outdoor sculpture garden, the centerpiece of which is Auguste Rodin's *Burghers of Calais*. Jefferson Drive continues past the National Air and Space Museum, which has indoor and outdoor cafés, and the Botanical Gardens.

15.0 *At the end of Jefferson Drive, cross First Street SW and enter the Capitol grounds, climbing Capitol Hill. At the top of the hill, bear right and exit the grounds at the corner of First Street SE and Independence Avenue. Turn left onto Independence Avenue.*

15.6 *Independence Avenue veers left. Keep right onto Pennsylvania Avenue SE.*

On your right are the Chesapeake Bagel Bakery and Sherrill's

Bakery, both good, informal eating places. In the next block are a fast-food-chain restaurant, a Thai-Italian restaurant, a Greek taverna, and other food establishments.

16.0 Eastern Market Metro station is on your right, at the corner of Pennsylvania Avenue and Seventh Street SE.

Bicycle Repair Service

Metropolis Bike and Scooter, 719 Eighth Street SE (202-543-8900)

3
Cycling around Capitol Hill

Location: The northeast and southeast quadrants of the District of Columbia

Metro access: Union Station

Terrain: Mainly flat

Road conditions: Paved roads, mainly with light traffic

Distance: 6.6 miles

Highlights: Union Station, the Capitol, the Library of Congress, Christ Church, the Gary Hart house, Eastern Market, Philadelphia Row, Congressional Cemetery, the Folger Library and Theatre

In Pierre L'Enfant's grand plan for Washington, the city was supposed to grow eastward from the Capitol, which is one reason the Statue of Freedom atop the Capitol dome faces east. Had things happened as L'Enfant envisioned them, the quiet neighborhood known before the construction of the Capitol as Jenkins Hill would probably have been obliterated. But since commercial and fancy residential development traveled west from the Capitol, Jenkins Hill survives, although it is now called Capitol Hill. This tour, which may be combined with Tour 1 (monuments) or Tour 2 (waterfront), takes you from monumental Washington to small-town Washington. En route, you'll see places where famous, infamous, and ordinary Washingtonians have lived, worshipped, shopped, and died.

The tour begins at Union Station, which has both a Metro station and a parking lot, as well as shops and restaurants.

0.0 *Leave Union Station, crossing Massachusetts Avenue in the pedestrian crosswalk in front of the Columbus fountain. Continue up Delaware Avenue.*

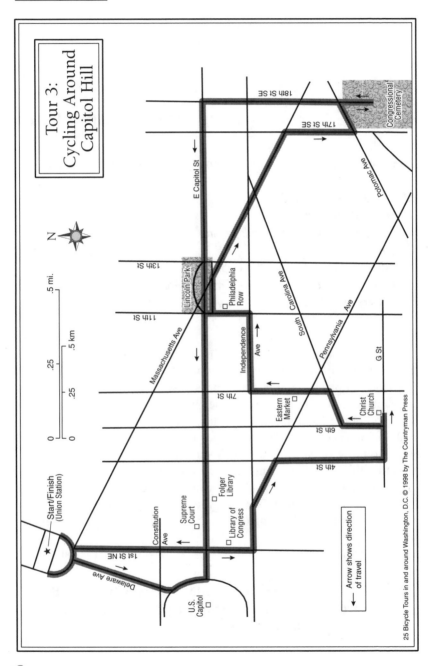

Tour 3:
Cycling Around
Capitol Hill

25 Bicycle Tours in and around Washington, D.C. © 1998 by The Countryman Press

Arrow shows direction
of travel

0.4 Cross Constitution Avenue and enter the Capitol grounds.

There are bike racks on either side of the building if you want to take a tour or just look at the view of the Mall from the West Terrace.

0.5 In front of the dome, turn left to the exit onto First Street NE. Then turn right onto First Street.

On your left is the Library of Congress's Jefferson Building. The ornate Renaissance architecture alone makes the Jefferson Building well worth a visit, and it also features Gutenberg Bibles, Stradivarius instruments, and changing exhibitions. The Court of Neptune Fountain, in front of the building, is reminiscent of Rome's Fountain of Trevi.

0.6 Turn left onto Independence Avenue

You're in front of the library's contemporary Madison Building, which also offers changing exhibits.

Just past the Madison Building, bear right onto Pennsylvania Avenue.

Here you'll find several shops and restaurants. Sherrill's Bakery, at 233 Pennsylvania Avenue SE, was the subject of a documentary film that was nominated for an Oscar.

1.0 Turn right onto Fourth Street, which has a marked bike lane.

1.3 Turn left onto G Street.

1.5 On your left is Christ Church.

The church was designed by Capitol architect Benjamin Latrobe in 1805 in the Gothic Revival style. Presidents Jefferson, Madison, and John Quincy Adams worshiped here and, much later, John Philip Sousa conducted the choir.

Turn around and double back half a block to Sixth Street. Turn right onto Sixth Street.

1.6 The house at 517 Sixth Street (left) is the one to which the press tracked Gary Hart and Donna Rice.

1.7 Turn right onto South Carolina Avenue.

On your left, at 630 South Carolina Avenue, stands The Maples, built in 1795 and once the home of Francis Scott Key. It is now a settlement house.

1.8 Turn left onto Seventh Street and cross Pennsylvania Avenue.

1.9 On your left is the Eastern Market, built in 1871 and the last of three such markets envisioned under the L'Enfant plan.

The market holds vegetable, meat, bakery, and fish stands and a restaurant noted for its crabcakes and blueberry pancakes. On Saturdays, farmers sell produce outside the market, competing for space with vendors of crafts and clothing. On Sundays, an active flea market springs up outside. The north end of the market houses an art gallery. Across Seventh Street are restaurants, food shops, antiques shops, and other stores.

2.0 Turn right onto Independence Avenue.

2.3 Turn left onto 11th Street.

The flat-fronted, Greek Revival–style houses on the right side of the street are known collectively as Philadelphia Row. They were designed in 1856 by George Gessford in the style of his native city.

2.4 Turn right onto East Capitol Street, which skirts Lincoln Park.

2.6 At the end of the park, bear right onto Massachusetts Avenue SE.

3.1 Turn right onto 17th Street SE.

3.4 Turn left onto Potomac Avenue to the entrance to Congressional Cemetery.

According to art historian James Goode, the cemetery has "the most historic collection of funeral sculpture in the city." Established in 1807 and partially supported by Congressional appropriations, it predated Arlington as a national cemetery. Every member of Congress who died between 1807 and 1877 was memorialized—though not necessarily buried—here by massive, Egyptian-like sandstone monuments designed by Benjamin Latrobe. The practice was stopped after one lawmaker, in a speech from the floor, said that the prospect of being buried under one of these "added terror to death." You can get a map at the gatekeeper's house or consult one posted outside. Of particular interest are the graves of Civil War photographer Mathew Brady, John Philip Sousa, J. Edgar Hoover, architect of the Capitol William Thornton, several Indian chiefs who died while visiting Washington, and

Begun in 1793 when George Washington laid the cornerstone, the U.S. Capitol was finished under Lincoln, who called its completion "a sign we intend the Union shall go on."

Elbridge Gerry. Lincoln came here in 1864 to the funeral of 21 young women workers killed in a Civil War arsenal explosion. They are buried under a monument paid for by donations from Washingtonians.

4.4 At the cemetery gate, cross Potomac Avenue and continue straight on 18th Street SE.

4.8 Turn left onto East Capitol Street.

5.1 On your right is an old trolley car barn that has been turned into condominiums.

Look straight ahead for a view of the Capitol dome with the Washington Monument jutting up behind it.

5.3 East Capitol Street turns right to skirt Lincoln Park.

Cross 13th Street and walk through the park to view the Mary McLeod Bethune Memorial, built to honor that black educator. You'll also see the Emancipation Monument, the city's first statue of Lincoln, built in 1876 with money donated by freed slaves.

5.5 Exit the park at East Capitol and 11th Streets. Cross 11th Street in the pedestrian crosswalk and continue west on East Capitol Street, which is framed by an arch of old elms.

After the trees have lost their leaves, there's a good view of the Capitol from here. The stately old homes that line the street were built from the 1840s to the early 1900s. In the 1870s, the city began permitting houses with bays. Before that time, houses had to have flat fronts—even now the city technically owns everything up to your front door (even the stoop)—in the older sections of the city. So it's a good bet that the Federal-style, flat-fronted houses with the ornate eyebrows over the windows are pre-1870. The houses with bays and intricate brickwork show the influence of the Queen Anne style and date from the 1870s to the 1930s. The Columbia Exposition, held in Chicago in 1893, ushered in a neoclassical revival, so houses built in the late 1890s and early 1900s usually lack intricate brickwork and ornamental detail. Tapestry bricks and red-tile roofing are a clue that a house was built in the 20th century. You'll find examples of all these architectural styles, and others, on East Capitol Street.

6.1 On your left is the Folger Shakespeare Library and Theatre.

The Great Hall offers changing exhibits, and admission is free. Bas-relief panels on the facade of the building depict scenes from Shakespeare.

6.2 On your right is the U.S. Supreme Court.

Visitors may tour the courtroom when the court is not sitting, and there is a small museum in the basement. When the court is in session, visitors must line up to be admitted for short periods.

Turn right in front of the court onto First Street NE.

6.6 Cross Massachusetts Avenue NE and enter Union Station.

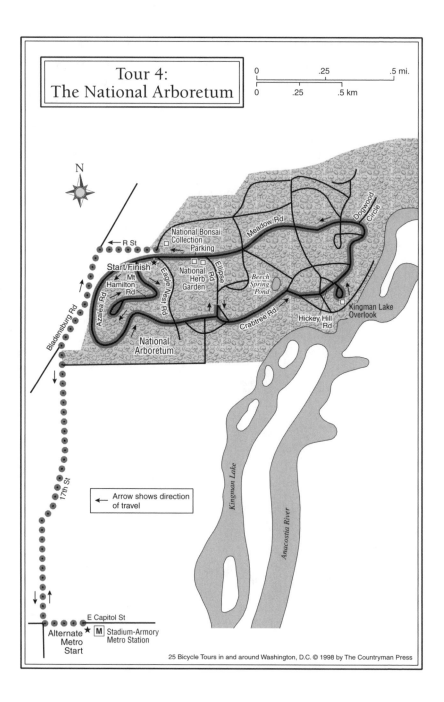

Tour 4:
The National Arboretum

0   .25   .5 mi.
0   .25   .5 km

N

R St

National Bonsai
Collection Parking

Start/Finish

Mt
Hamilton
Rd

Azalea Rd

Eagle Nest Rd

National
Herb
Garden

Ellipse
Rd

Meadow Rd

Dogwood
Circle

Beech
Spring
Pond

Crabtree Rd

Hickey Hill
Rd

Kingman Lake
Overlook

Bladensburg Rd

National
Arboretum

17th St

Arrow shows direction
of travel

Kingman Lake

Anacostia River

E Capitol St

Alternate
Metro
Start

M Stadium-Armory
Metro Station

25 Bicycle Tours in and around Washington, D.C. © 1998 by The Countryman Press

4
The National Arboretum

Location: *The northeast quadrant of the District of Columbia*
Metro access: *Alternate start at Stadium-Armory Metro Station*
Terrain: *Rolling hills*
Road conditions: *Busy city streets outside the arboretum. Inside the arboretum, all roads are paved and traffic is light except during peak spring viewing times. (See below.)*
Distance: *5 miles if you start from the arboretum parking lot, 9 miles if you start from Stadium-Armory Metro station*
Highlights: *A delightful sampling of gardens, trees, and views*

The main purpose of the 444-acre National Arboretum is to facilitate government research on trees, shrubs, and herbaceous plants, but it's also a boon to bicyclists who want to take a short, refreshing country ride without leaving the city. You can stop and look at everything or just breeze on through, smelling the blossoms as you pass. Here's a rough idea of what you'll smell—and see—when:

Late March–mid-April: Daffodils, magnolias, camellias, quince, rhododendrons, flowering cherries, crab apples

Late April–May: Azaleas, dogwoods, mountain laurel, peonies, old roses, wildflowers, lilacs

June–August: Day lilies, lilies, waterlilies, crape myrtles, herbs

September–October: Deciduous trees put on a fall color show, even the dwarf trees in the Bonsai Collection.

For a Metro start, use Stadium-Armory station, 2 miles away. From the station, turn left onto East Capitol Street, then right onto 17th Street NE to the intersection with Bladensburg Road. Bear right onto Bladensburg and continue to R Street NE. Turn right onto R Street and proceed to the entrance. There is also a large parking lot if you want to drive to the

Arboretum. The mileage count begins in the parking lot. Pick up maps and brochures in the Administration Building next to the parking lot before you start.

0.0 *Exit the parking lot and turn right onto Azalea Road.*

0.2 *Turn left onto Mount Hamilton Road.*

This road winds up through azaleas, rhododendrons, and may-apples to the top of 239-foot Mount Hamilton. Rest on the bench at the top of the "mountain" and drink in the view of the Capitol, the Library of Congress, the Washington Monument, the Washington Cathedral, and the Shrine of the Immaculate Conception.

0.6 *Proceed down the mountain and back to Azalea Road.*

1.0 *Go left onto Azalea Road.*

On your left you'll see azalea-strewn Mount Hamilton; on your right, crab apple trees. The Morrison Azalea Garden, at the intersection with Eagle Nest Road, features a study collection of large-flowered Japanese hybrids. After the intersection, Azalea Road becomes Crabtree Road.

2.1 *Turn left onto Ellipse Road.*

Here you'll find a majestic and picturesque "ruin" created from the Corinthian columns removed from the U.S. Capitol during renovation of the east front during the Kennedy administration. The 14-ton columns were designed by Benjamin Latrobe. Set on this hill and surrounded by understated gardens, they form the closest thing to the Acropolis this side of Athens.

Return to Crabtree Road.

2.9 *Fern Valley is on your left.*

It features a self-guided nature trail along a stream, over a bridge, and past witch hazel, ferns, oaks, wild ginger, bloodroot, trilliums, Dutchman's breeches, stunted American chestnuts, mountain laurel, and hemlocks. Lock your bike in the rack provided.

3.1 *Beech Spring Pond is home to ducks and other waterfowl. Its banks are lined with weeping willows. Don't take the road that skirts the pond. Instead, bear right onto Hickey Hill Road. Then continue on Hickey Hill Road.*

Corinthian columns removed from the east front of the Capitol
grace a hill in the 444-acre National Arboretum.

3.3 *Take the overlook loop (right) to the Kingman Lake Overlook
high above the Anacostia River.*

3.5 *Lock your bike in the rack here.*

Take the path through the camellias and the Asian collections to
the cinnabar Chinese teahouse, which overlooks a man-made
waterfall cascading into the Anacostia River. There's a rest room
and a drinking fountain near the bike rack.

3.5 Follow Hickey Hill Road as it curves to the left.

4.0 Park your bike in the rack adjacent to Dogwood Circle.

Stroll down the trail that winds through the woods here. Then walk across the road to the Gotelli Dwarf and Slow-Growing Conifer Collection, about 1,500 tiny trees in a landscaped setting.

4.0 Back on your bike, follow Meadow Road down the hill, past the crape myrtles (left), past Heart Pond, named for its shape (right), over the bridge that spans Hickey Run.

4.7 Just past the intersection with Ellipse Road, stop to tour the National Bonsai Collection on your right.

A Bicentennial gift from Japan, some of the tiny trees are hundreds of years old. There are both evergreen and deciduous trees in the collection. The latter lose their leaves in the fall, just as big trees do. The National Herb Garden, on your left, is a fascinating collection of herbs used for medicinal and culinary purposes. In the same area is a collection of old roses.

5.0 Return to the parking lot.

Bicycle Repair Service

Metropolis Bike and Scooter, 719 Eighth Street SE (202-543-8900)

5
Tenleytown Trot

Location: Northwest Washington
Metro access: Start: Tenleytown. Finish: Foggy Bottom.
Terrain: Mainly downhill and flat
Road conditions: A paved, off-road bike trail and (mainly) light-traffic streets
Distance: 8.4 miles
Highlights: The pleasantly upscale Washington neighborhoods of Tenleytown, Spring Valley, Wesley Heights, and Palisades; spectacular views of the Potomac River, the Capital Crescent Trail, the Georgetown waterfront

By using Metro—or by planting cars at both ends of this trip—you can cheat Washington's geography and enjoy a mainly downhill ride. The tour starts at the Tenleytown Metro stop, situated in the shadow of the city's highest natural point, in Fort Reno Park. It then begins a downhill slope through the American University Park neighborhood that surrounds the institution of the same name, crosses into the posher quarters of Spring Valley, and then goes into the funkier but still upscale Palisades area. After a ride along the street on the edge of the palisades above the Potomac, the tour joins the Capital Crescent Trail and follows the river into Georgetown. The tour ends at the Foggy Bottom Metro station.

0.0 *Exit the Tenleytown Metro station via the elevator and cross Albemarle Street NW and Wisconsin Avenue NW at the lights. Proceed south on Wisconsin Avenue.*

0.1 *Turn right onto Yuma Street, in front of St. Anne's Catholic Church.*

   The Oakcrest School will be on your right and an annex of

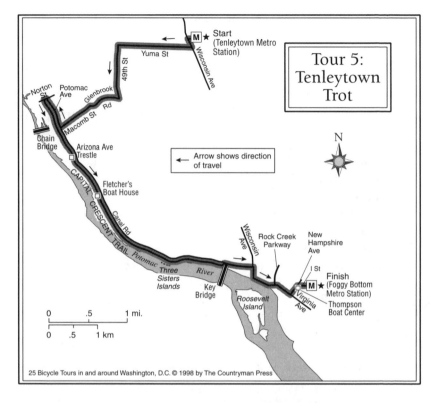

Tour 5:
Tenleytown
Trot

N

Arrow shows direction
of travel

25 Bicycle Tours in and around Washington, D.C. © 1998 by The Countryman Press

American University on your left. Yuma Street is lined with neat, brick Colonial-style homes and goes steadily downhill.

1.0 At the bottom of the hill, turn left onto 49th Street.

Just before 49th Street crosses Massachusetts Avenue NW, look to your left at the small shopping center. Wagshall's Market there makes excellent sandwiches. After crossing Massachusetts Avenue, there's another opportunity for refreshment at Sutton Place Gourmet (left). You are now in Spring Valley, one of Washington's most upscale neighborhoods.

1.5 49th Street dead-ends. Turn right onto Glenbrook Road, a heavily treed street with large, sprawling houses set back from the road.

The road goes downhill, then up, crosses busy Loughboro Road, then heads downhill again.

Bear left onto Macomb Street and continue downhill into the Palisades neighborhood.

2.6 **Cross busy MacArthur Boulevard.**

This artery was originally called Conduit Road because of the aqueducts that ran underneath, carrying Washington's water supply. It was renamed for the World War II hero.

3.0 **Macomb Street dead-ends at Potomac Avenue, at the edge of the palisades that tower over the river.**

Relatively modest homes with million-dollar views sit on the east side of the street, leaving the river side open. From here, you can gaze down on a three-tiered view. Just below you is the Capital Crescent Trail, replete with in-line skaters, strollers, and cyclists. Below that, separated by woods, are the C&O Canal and towpath. And below that, the Potomac rolls over boulders and dams into Washington.

Turn right onto Potomac Avenue.

3.5 **Potomac Avenue dead-ends at Norton Avenue, in front of the Dalecarlia Reservoir. Follow the well-worn dirt path next to the reservoir fence, which leads to the Capital Crescent Trail. Turn left onto this paved trail, the area's newest rails-to-trails product (see Tour 6).**

4.5 **The trail crosses the Arizona Avenue Trestle, a 19th-century engineering wonder.**

Look down at the C&O Canal and towpath. After traversing the trestle bridge, the trail runs side by side with the towpath, and many people cross from one to the other.

5.0 **Fletcher's Boat House offers rest rooms and refreshments.**

On your left, accessible by crossing the canal on a footbridge, stands the Abner Cloud House, built in 1801. The Clouds lived upstairs and used the basement to store grain and flour from a nearby mill he operated. The trail continues, veering slightly downhill and getting close to the river.

6.5 **In mid-river, look for the Three Sisters Islands, favorite haunts of recreational boaters.**

In the early 1970s, a plan to build a bridge at this point was

The multiuse Capital Crescent Trail has brought new life to an abandoned rail spur that once carried fuel, building supplies, and other freight between Georgetown and Silver Spring.

defeated by conservationists. Look downriver for views of the Key Bridge, the Rosslyn skyline, and the Kennedy Center for the Performing Arts.

7.1 *The Capital Crescent Trail ends near the ruins of the old Aqueduct Bridge in Georgetown.*

Built in 1843, the bridge carried barges across the river to another canal that led to the port of Alexandria. In 1886, it was converted to an automobile bridge, and in 1933 it was replaced by the nearby Key Bridge.

Continue in the same direction on K Street, a formerly industrial area of Georgetown, under the elevated Whitehurst Freeway.

7.5 *At Wisconsin Avenue (left), turn right toward the waterfront, then left along a gravel path that leads to the glitzy Washington Harbor development.*

Walk your bike along the sometimes crowded walkway, past restaurants and shops. In mid-river (right) lies Theodore Roosevelt Island, a wildlife sanctuary dedicated to the conservationist president.

Just before Thompson Boat Center, turn left into the parking lot for the same facility. Cross Rock Creek Parkway at the light and continue up Virginia Avenue.

You'll pass the notorious Watergate complex, venue of the break-in that eventually toppled Nixon and residence of intern fatale Monica Lewinsky.

8.1 *Turn left onto New Hampshire Avenue. Turn right onto the I Street pedestrian mall.*

Enter the Foggy Bottom Metro station via the elevator.

Bicycle Repair Service

Washington Bike Center, 4445 Wisconsin Avenue NW (202-363-7590)

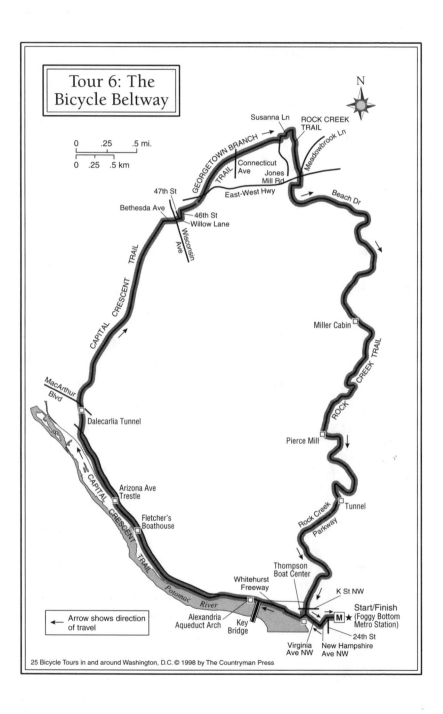

Tour 6: The Bicycle Beltway

N

| 0 | .25 | .5 mi. |
| 0 | .25 | .5 km |

Susanna Ln
ROCK CREEK TRAIL
GEORGETOWN BRANCH
Meadowbrook Ln
Connecticut Ave
Jones Mill Rd
TRAIL
47th St
East-West Hwy
Beach Dr
Bethesda Ave
46th St
Willow Lane
Wisconsin Ave
CAPITAL CRESCENT TRAIL
Miller Cabin
ROCK CREEK TRAIL
MacArthur Blvd
Dalecarlia Tunnel
Pierce Mill
ROCK
Arizona Ave Trestle
CAPITAL CRESCENT TRAIL
Fletcher's Boathouse
Tunnel
Rock Creek Parkway
Thompson Boat Center
Potomac River
Whitehurst Freeway
K St NW
Start/Finish
(Foggy Bottom Metro Station)
Alexandria Aqueduct Arch
Key Bridge
M ★
24th St
Virginia Ave NW
New Hampshire Ave NW

Arrow shows direction of travel

25 Bicycle Tours in and around Washington, D.C. © 1998 by The Countryman Press

The Bicycle Beltway

Location: Northwest D.C. and Montgomery County, Maryland
Metro access: Foggy Bottom
Terrain: Gentle uphill climb at the start, then flat or downhill
Road conditions: Paved off-road bike trails, a gravel off-road bike trail with a few "portages" on suburban streets
Distance: 21.4 miles
Highlights: The Potomac River, the Dalecarlia Tunnel and Reservoir, Bethesda restaurants, the Montgomery Farm Women's Cooperative, Rock Creek Park

To motorists, "the Beltway" connotes gridlock, heartburn, and road rage. But bicyclists now have a very different kind of beltway, a pastoral, tree-shaded, scenic inner loop that links Georgetown with Bethesda and then ambles back to town through bucolic Rock Creek Park. The 21-mile loop begins at the Foggy Bottom Metro station, accesses the Georgetown waterfront through the Thompson Boat Center, then enters the Capital Crescent Trail, a paved, multiuse pathway built along the abandoned Georgetown Branch, a railway spur completed in 1910 to link Georgetown with the main B&O line at Silver Spring. After crossing downtown Bethesda on city streets—with tempting opportunities to stop for lunch—the tour continues on an interim, gravel trail called the Georgetown Branch Trail, then connects with the Rock Creek Trail for a trip that follows that babbling brook back to the starting point.

0.0 Exit the Foggy Bottom Metro station, turning left. Cross 24th Street and turn left onto New Hampshire Avenue NW.

0.1 Turn right onto Virginia Avenue NW.

0.3 Cross Rock Creek Parkway at the light and enter Thompson

Boat Center, where rental bikes are available. Go through the parking lot and turn left along the waterfront, walking your bike in front of the trendy restaurants.

The walkway will lead you to K Street NW, under the Whitehurst Freeway.

Turn left onto K Street.

Some parking is available here on Sundays.

0.7 *After passing under the Key Bridge and the Alexandria Aqueduct Arch, the remains of an 1,100-foot aqueduct that once carried boats from the C&O Canal across the Potomac into Virgina, enter the Capital Crescent Trail.*

The trail is paved and popular not only with cyclists but also with in-line skaters, dog walkers, and families with strollers. At the outset, it parallels the C&O Canal towpath, running between the canal and the river.

2.8 *Fletcher's Boat House (left) offers refreshments and rest rooms. Parking and bike rentals are also available here.*

3.3 *The Arizona Avenue Trestle carries the trail over the canal and Canal Road.*

According to the trail brochure, the trestle spans are "outstanding examples of 19th-century pin-connected Whipple trapezoidal design." Past this point, the trail starts curving east, away from the river and toward Bethesda.

4.8 *The Dalecarlia Tunnel, completed in 1910, carries the trail under MacArthur Boulevard.*

Note the decorative brick facing at both ends. As you emerge, look to your right for a view of the Dalecarlia Reservoir, a key link in Washington's water supply. The trail continues beside Little Falls, a stream destined for the Potomac.

6.0 *On your right is a marker for the site of Loughborough Mill.*

One Nathan Loughborough came to the Federal City from Philadelphia in 1800, looking for work. He built a flour mill at this location in 1830, using the wheat that arrived in Georgetown on the canal barges. Loughborough Road is named for this family,

A cyclist checks the map at the Georgetown entrance to the Capital Crescent Trail, a paved pathway that links Georgetown, Bethesda, Silver Spring, and the Rock Creek Hiker-Biker Trail.

which fled south during the Civil War.

7.8 *After crossing River Road on a bridge and biking through the backyards of Bethesda, the trail ends—for the moment—at Bethesda Avenue in the heart of downtown Bethesda.*

Restaurant choices abound here. The Thyme Square Café, at 4735 Bethesda Avenue, emphasizes vegetarian haute cuisine.

The Capital Crescent Trail Coalition is lobbying Montgomery County to open an existing railroad tunnel under Wisconsin Avenue, connecting the two segments of the trail. At press time the tunnel was not open.

Follow the signs that read GEORGETOWN BRANCH TRAIL *up Bethesda Avenue to the intersection with Wisconsin Avenue. Cross Wisconsin in front of the Montgomery Farm Women's Cooperative.*

On Wednesday and Saturday, there's a farmer's market here. On Sunday, there's a flea market.

7.9 *Just past the market, turn right onto Willow Lane.*

8.0 *Turn left onto 47th Street and ride through the Elm Street Park, turning right at the sign onto the trail.*

The trail, packed gravel, goes downhill through woods and meadows and traverses the Columbia Country Club.

9.2 *The trail emerges at Connecticut Avenue. Cross Connecticut at the light and turn left.*

9.3 *Reenter the trail between an Exxon station and a bank.*

10.0 *The trail emerges at Jones Mill Road. Turn left onto Jones Mill, then right onto Susanna Lane.*

10.2 *Turn right onto the Rock Creek Trail, which follows the stream into a park with athletic fields and playgrounds.*

10.9 *Cross East-West Highway and enter Meadowbrook Lane.*

11.0 *On your right are the Meadowbrook Stables.*

Ride around the stables, bearing left alongside the playground. There are rest rooms in the log house next to the playground.

11.1 *Cross the footbridge in front of the log house and turn left onto Beach Drive.*

12.2 *Beach Drive crosses the District line.*

In the District, Beach Drive is closed to cars on weekends. It winds through the park, beside the ever-widening creek. Picnic groves, available to groups by reservation, line the road.

15.0 On your right is the log Miller Cabin.

Built by rough-hewn Joaquin Miller, "The Poet of the Sierras," the cabin originally stood in Meridian Hill Park on 16th Street, but was moved here courtesy of the California State Society. Poetry readings are held here on occasion.

16.6 Enter the off-road trail to your right.

16.8 Pierce Mill, the sole survivor of 26 gristmills powered by Rock Creek, stands on your right.

Rest rooms and drinking fountains are available here.

18.3 The trail comes to a tunnel. Detour to the right on a wooded trail through the zoo grounds.

18.8 Rejoin the main trail.

20.1 The slope on your right is part of Oak Hill Cemetery.

The cemetery is the final resting place of many of Washington's elite, from "Home, Sweet Home" author John Payne to *Washington Post* publisher Philip Graham. The white-columned memorial modeled after Rome's Temple of Vesta is the tomb of Marcia Burns Van Ness, who died in the devastating cholera epidemic of 1832. There is no access to the cemetery from the trail.

20.2 The trail passes under the Buffalo Bridge. Look up at the sandstone faces of an Indian on the arch. The face was reportedly modeled on the death mask of Sitting Bull.

21.1 At Thompson Boat Center, cross Rock Creek Parkway with the light and continue up Virginia Avenue.

21.3 Turn left onto New Hampshire Avenue.

21.4 Cross 24th Street and enter the Foggy Bottom Metro station to your right.

Bicycle Repair Service

The Bicycle Place, Inc., 10219 Old Georgetown Road, Bethesda, MD (301-530-0100)

Griffin Cycle Inc, 4949 Bethesda Avenue, Bethesda, MD (301-656-6188)

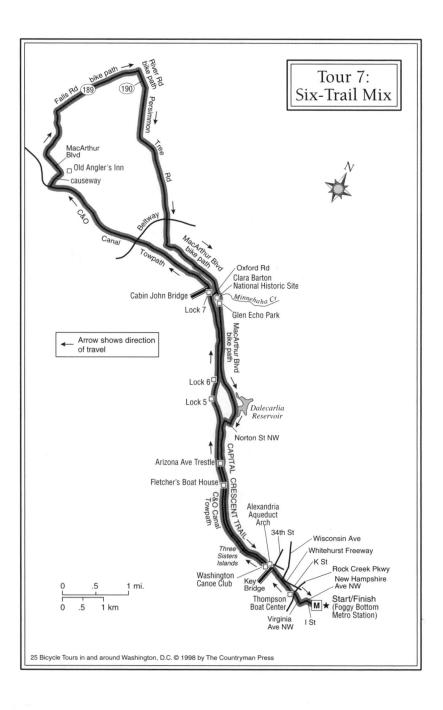

Tour 7:
Six-Trail Mix

Falls Rd
River Rd bike path
189
190
bike path
Persimmon

Tree Rd

MacArthur Blvd
Old Angler's Inn
causeway

C&O Canal
Beltway
Towpath
MacArthur Blvd bike path

Oxford Rd
Clara Barton National Historic Site
Cabin John Bridge
Minnehaha Cr.
Lock 7
Glen Echo Park

MacArthur Blvd bike path

Arrow shows direction of travel

Lock 6
Lock 5
Dalecarlia Reservoir

Norton St NW

CAPITAL CRESCENT TRAIL

Arizona Ave Trestle
Fletcher's Boat House

C&O Canal Towpath

Alexandria Aqueduct Arch
34th St
Wisconsin Ave
Whitehurst Freeway
K St
Rock Creek Pkwy
New Hampshire Ave NW
Three Sisters Islands
Washington Canoe Club
Key Bridge
Thompson Boat Center
Virginia Ave NW
I St
M ★ Start/Finish
(Foggy Bottom Metro Station)

0   .5   1 mi.
0   .5   1 km

25 Bicycle Tours in and around Washington, D.C. © 1998 by The Countryman Press

7
Six-Trail Mix

Location: *Northwest Washington and Montgomery County, Maryland*
Metro access: *Foggy Bottom*
Terrain: *Mainly flat, with a few short uphill climbs*
Road conditions: *A hard-packed dirt trail, paved off-road and on-road trails, light-traffic streets*
Distance: *33.4 miles*
Highlights: *The Chesapeake and Ohio Canal towpath with locks and lockhouses; the Old Angler's Inn; upscale Potomac, Maryland, with shops, restaurants, and country clubs; the Clara Barton Historic Site; Glen Echo Park; the Capital Crescent Trail; the Georgetown waterfront*

This tour, which starts at the Foggy Bottom Metro station, makes use of six—count 'em, six—area bicycle trails. After a very brief ride on the Rock Creek Trail, it follows the granddaddy of all multiuse trails, the C&O Canal towpath, through leafy Georgetown and past the Beltway. It stops for an al fresco lunch at the fashionable Old Angler's Inn, and after a short stint on the on-road MacArthur Boulevard bicycle trail, it follows the off-road Falls Road bicycle trail into the center of horsey Potomac and onto the River Road off-road bicycle trail. The tour then swoops down Persimmon Tree Road, lined with million-dollar homes and country clubs, into the funkier but still classy Carderock neighborhood, and rejoins the MacArthur Boulevard trail, which leads past the restored home of Clara Barton and Glen Echo Park, an art deco–era amusement park turned arts center. After crossing the District line, the tour picks up the Capital Crescent Trail for a final descent back to the starting point.

    0.0 *Exit the Foggy Bottom Metro station via the elevator and turn right onto the I Street pedestrian mall. At the intersection, turn left onto New Hampshire Avenue, which still has some of the*

Victorian row houses of the old Foggy Bottom district.

This is what the whole neighborhood looked like before George Washington University and high-rise apartment houses encroached.

0.2 Turn right onto Virginia Avenue NW.

On your left is the Watergate complex, site of the infamous burglary that felled a president.

0.4 Cross Rock Creek Parkway in the pedestrian crossing and turn right on the Rock Creek bike path.

0.7 Across the parkway, on your right, stand the ruins of the Godey Lime Kilns, which processed lime brought to Georgetown on the Chesapeake and Ohio Canal from western quarries. Turn left into the C&O Canal towpath.

The Chesapeake and Ohio Canal, begun in 1828, stretches from the mouth of Rock Creek in Georgetown to Cumberland, Maryland, some 185 miles to the northwest. An elevated towpath, built 12 feet wide to accommodate the mule teams that pulled the canal barges, now accommodates hikers, joggers, horseback riders—and cyclists.

Follow the paved towpath through Georgetown.

You'll pass four lift locks, the embarkation point for the mule-powered boat that takes visitors on short canal rides, and some old brick houses now painted in rainbow colors and used as artists' studios and shops. One offers carryout food and ice-cream cones.

1.6 At 34th Street, the towpath crosses the canal on a bridge and becomes a dirt trail.

Here the canal is lined with old warehouses and industrial buildings that have been turned into smart shops and condominiums.

1.7 After passing under Key Bridge, you'll see the Victorian-style clubhouse of the Washington Canoe Club on your left.

Busy Canal Road is on your right across the canal. Just beyond this point, Canal Road ceases to be a major thoroughfare, and the towpath becomes quieter, more countrylike.

3.8 On your left is Fletcher's Boat House.

It offers bike, canoe, and boat rentals and a snack bar. There are picnic tables and a pleasant lawn that leads down to a cove on the Potomac River.

4.5 *Cross a wooden bridge over a canal spillway.*

5.7 *At Lock #5, the towpath crosses a bridge. Rest rooms and a drinking fountain are available here.*

6.1 *The small, whitewashed house provided for the tender of Lock #6 is typical of these four-room residences, which were part of the compensation for the tenders.*

A one-acre garden plot came with the house. In addition, the canal company paid a salary that ranged from $100 a year to $75 a month. Boats signaled the tender with a bugle. In the canal's heyday in the 1870s, an average of more than a hundred boats a day passed through the locks. In 1835 the canal company's board ruled against hiring women to tend locks, feeling that the work was too strenuous. An exception was made for Elizabeth Burgess, who was hired to tend Lock #2 "providing that she hire a capable assistant."

In this area, the towpath stays close to the Potomac River, affording views of Little Falls Dam just upstream. Heed the posted warnings about staying out of the dangerous river.

7.1 *On your left is the private Sycamore Island Club.*

7.8 *A wooden footbridge on your right is a good vantage point to watch turtles sunning themselves on the rocks below.*

10.1 *Just after passing Lock #7, the towpath goes under the Cabin John Bridge.*

On your right after the bridge is the David Taylor Model Basin, used by the Navy to test the seaworthiness of ship designs. On your left is a large picnic area.

13.1 *A wide causeway to your right leads to the Old Anglers Inn on MacArthur Boulevard.*

During one of his celebrated hikes to save the canal from being paved over to create a highway, Justice William O. Douglas stopped here, with fellow canal aficionados, for lunch. Since the hikers were not dressed in proper restaurant attire, the management turned them away. Now, however, the restaurant accommodates hikers and cyclists with tables placed outside, although the menu is pricey.

After lunch, continue heading west on the signed—but on-road—MacArthur Boulevard trail.

The hills on this short stretch will work off anything you had for lunch.

14.1 *Turn right onto Falls Road (MD 189), entering the bike path on the right side of the road.*

The path, largely shielded from the road by trees and other vegetation, leads through the tracts of million-dollar homes that make up Potomac, Maryland.

16.1 *The bike path ends just before the intersection with River Road (MD 190).*

There is a shopping center with carryout and restaurant food available.

Cross River Road and Falls Road in the pedestrian crossings and turn right onto River Road, entering the bicycle path that begins just past the gas station and the bank.

17.0 *At the standing clock, turn right onto Persimmon Tree Road, which curves downhill past expensive homes and exclusive country clubs.*

After crossing the Beltway on a bridge, you enter the funkier Carderock neighborhood and descend to MacArthur Boulevard.

20.9 *Turn left onto the MacArthur Boulevard bike path.*

22.0 *Turn right onto Oxford Road to the Clara Barton National Historic Site.*

The pleasant, yellow-clapboard house was built in 1891, of boards salvaged by the Red Cross from the great flood in Johnstown, Pennsylvania. It served as both home and office for American Red Cross founder Clara Barton, who got her start when, as a Patent Office clerk, she volunteered for duty in the field hospital set up in that office during the Civil War. After the war, she helped locate missing soldiers and lobbied for the adoption of the Geneva Convention. She retired to this house after a bitter bust-up with President Theodore Roosevelt over the Red Cross performance during the Spanish-American War, and died here in 1912.

Built in 1801, the Abner Cloud House is the oldest building
on the C&O Canal.

After visiting the Barton house, continue across the parking lot
to Glen Echo Park.

22.3 *Cross Minnehaha Creek on a wooden footbridge, and follow the path into Glen Echo Park.*

The first organized activity on this site began in 1891, with a
Chautauqua Assembly "to promote liberal and practical education
especially among the masses of the people," and, not incidentally,
to sell lots and houses to the same masses. The park was promoted
as the "Rhineland of the Potomac," but the bubble burst after

rumors of malaria surfaced. Later, the site was transformed into an amusement park, with rides, a ballroom, and the Crystal Pool, which held 3,000 people. The park closed in 1968, but most of the buildings still stand and the National Park Service runs the historic Dentzel Carousel. Art groups now occupy most of the buildings, but more change may be in store, as the National Park Service is reevaluating the use of the site.

22.6 *Passing to the left of the stone tower, the only building remaining from the Chautauqua period, carry your bike up a set of stone steps and turn right onto the MacArthur Boulevard bike path.*

22.7 *The charming Inn at Glen Echo, to your right, was formerly a roadhouse called Trav's, where generations of local teens carved their initials in wooden booths.*

23.4 *Continue on the bike trail past the Army mapping facility and the Dalecarlia Reservoir and across the District line.*

The old-fashioned Sycamore Store, across MacArthur Boulevard, sells sandwiches and bottled soft drinks.

25.7 *Just past the reservoir, turn right onto Norton Avenue NW.*

25.8 *Where Norton Avenue dead-ends, turn right onto a dirt path and walk your bike down to the Capital Crescent Trail.*

25.9 *Turn left onto the trail, which runs downhill toward the Potomac.*

Through the woods to your right, you can catch glimpses of the C&O Canal and towpath and the river.

26.8 *The trail crosses Canal Road and the canal on the Arizona Avenue trestle.*

This double-span bridge is supposed to be a superb example of 19th-century pin-connected Whipple trapezoidal design.

30.0 *Fletcher's Boat House is on your right.*

The Boat House rents bikes and boats, sells refreshments, and offers rest rooms. Picnic tables and fishing spots are available along the Potomac. On your left stands the Abner Cloud House, the oldest along the canal. The trail and the towpath run side by side for a stretch. Watch for traffic crossing from one to the other.

31.5 On the river, to your right, look for three rocky islets, known as the Three Sisters.

Plans to build a bridge at this spot were thwarted in the 1970s by conservationists.

32.1 The trail ends at the ruins of the Alexandria Aqueduct Arch.

The aqueduct once carried barges from the canal across the river and onward, by another canal, to the port of Alexandria. The aqueduct bridge was torn down in 1933 and replaced by the adjacent Key Bridge, a vehicular bridge.

Continue on K Street, under the Whitehurst Freeway and along the Georgetown waterfront.

32.5 Across from Wisconsin Avenue, turn right onto a path that leads toward the waterfront.

Follow it into the Washington Harbor complex of restaurants and shops, where you will have to walk your bike.

32.8 Just before Thompson Boat Center, turn left and exit through the parking lot, crossing Rock Creek Parkway at the light and continuing on Virginia Avenue NW.

33.1 Turn left onto New Hampshire Avenue NW.

33.3 Turn right onto the I Street pedestrian mall.

33.4 Enter the Foggy Bottom Metro station via the elevator.

Bicycle Repair Service

The Bicycle Pro Shop, 3403 M Street NW, Washington, DC (202-337-0311)

8

Exploring Arlington Cemetery

Location: *Arlington County, Virginia*
Metro access: *Arlington Cemetery*
Terrain: *Hilly*
Road conditions: *Paved bike trails and low-traffic roads*
Distance: *3.0 miles*
Highlights: *Arlington Cemetery, Fort Myer, the Marine Corps War Memorial, the Netherlands Carillon*

This tour allows cyclists to take advantage of several types of federally owned land, including a national cemetery and a military installation. Although the distance pedaled is short, you may want to set aside enough time to take in the sights and wander on foot. It's particularly suitable for families because there are places to stop, things to see, and little danger from traffic.

The tour begins at the Arlington Cemetery stop. If you want to drive to the start, there is a pay parking lot at the Arlington Cemetery Visitors Center. Bike helmets are required, both in the cemetery and on Fort Myer.

0.0 *From the Metro elevator, cross Memorial Drive and enter the visitors center, where maps, rest rooms, and water fountains are available. When you exit the visitors center, turn left and continue to the end of Memorial Drive.*

0.1 *Turn right onto Schley Drive, which winds uphill, makes a left turn, and becomes Sherman Drive.*

No cars are permitted in the cemetery except those of bona fide relatives of people buried here, so traffic is very light.

0.2 *On the left is a walk leading to the grave of William Howard Taft and his wife, Helen.*

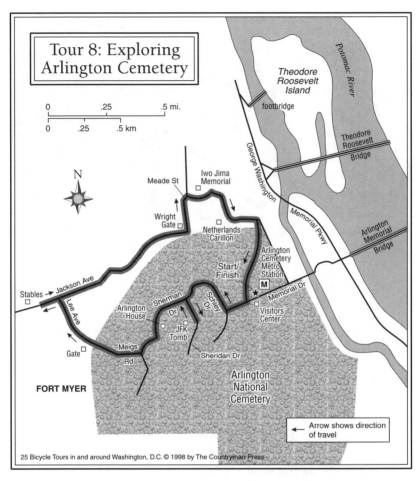

Tour 8: Exploring Arlington Cemetery

25 Bicycle Tours in and around Washington, D.C. © 1998 by The Countryman Press

An appropriately Edwardian memorial in ornate rose marble, it has shaded benches. Nearby are the starker graves of a whole generation of well-known military leaders: Omar Bradley, Lawton Collins, Earle Wheeler, for example.

0.3 At the intersection with Sheridan Drive, there's a bike rack and a water fountain.

Lock your bike here and walk down Sheridan Drive to the John F. Kennedy and Robert F. Kennedy grave sites. Then continue climbing the hill on Sherman Drive.

0.5 Turn left into the entrance for Arlington House.

French architect and city planner Major Pierre L'Enfant, the designer of Washington, is buried here on a ridge overlooking the city.

Before entering the house, walk to the edge of the bluff to the grave of Maj. Pierre L'Enfant, architect of the Federal City. Another Frenchman, the Marquis de Lafayette, described the view from here as the "finest view in the world." Built between 1802 and 1817 by George Washington Parke Custis, a descendant of Martha Washington, the house was named for the ancestral Custis estate on the eastern shore of Virginia. It passed to his daughter, Mary Anna Randolph Custis, who married a young West Point graduate named Robert E. Lee. It was here at Arlington House, in his bedroom on the second floor, on the night of April 19, 1861, that Lee made his painful and fateful decision to resign from the U.S. Army and join the Confederate forces. Two days later he left for Richmond, never to return to Arlington House. The estate was confiscated in 1864, and a military cemetery was started on the grounds. After the war, a descendant of the Lees sued the government for return of the property—and won. But since the military graves surrounding the house made it unattractive as a dwelling, he accepted a settlement of $150,000.

Of special interest in the mansion is the White Parlor. The decor of this room shows the influence of the time Lee spent in

Mexico during the Mexican-American War.

Exit the mansion driveway and turn left, continuing along Sherman Drive.

0.6 Turn right onto Meigs Drive.

This road was named for Maj. Gen. Montgomery Meigs, quartermaster general of the Union Army, whose idea it was to commandeer the Lee estate for a military cemetery. Meigs's vindictive attitude is made more understandable by the fact that his own son, Maj. John Rodgers Meigs, was killed at the age of 22 in a Virginia skirmish in 1864.

0.9 Pass through the gate to Fort Myer. Meigs Avenue becomes Lee Avenue at the gate. Follow it around to the right.

Just inside the gate, on the Fort Myer side, is a small chapel used for many of the funerals that culminate in burial in Arlington.

1.2 Turn left onto Jackson Avenue, in front of the Officers' Club. Continue past the post office.

On the right are the stables that house the horses used for military funerals and other ceremonies. They are open for free, informal tours daily from noon to 4.

1.3 Reverse direction and double back on Jackson Avenue, past the fine old redbrick homes of senior Army officers, and head downhill toward Wright Gate.

2.1 Just beyond the gate, turn left onto Meade Street, which leads to the Marine Corps War Memorial, known informally as the Iwo Jima monument.

The statue sets in bronze a photograph taken by Associated Press combat photographer Joe Rosenthal, a native Washingtonian. The Pulitzer Prize–winning picture showed six Marines raising the American flag atop Mount Suribachi, the highest point on the small island of Iwo Jima and the scene of bloody fighting in 1945. Three of those Marines survived the battle and later posed for sculptor Felix de Weldon. De Weldon sculpted likenesses of the three dead Marines from photographs.

Adjacent to the memorial is the Netherlands Carillon, a gift from the people of the Netherlands in recognition of our aid during

World War II.

2.3 *Turn right out of the parking lot for the Marine memorial and follow the path that leads in front of the carillon.*

The path turns left, then right, and runs between the red sandstone wall of the cemetery and the highway.

2.9 *At the intersection with Memorial Drive, turn left.*

3.0 *The Metro elevator is to your left.*

Bicycle Repair Service

Metropolis Bike and Scooter, The Village at Shirlington, Arlington, Virginia (703-671-1700)

Along the Potomac to Mount Vernon

Location: Northern Virginia
Metro access: Ronald Reagan National Airport
Terrain: Mostly flat with a few hills approaching Mount Vernon
Road conditions: A paved, off-the-road bike path except for a short
    stretch on city streets through Alexandria, where there will be light-to-
    moderate traffic on weekends
Distance: 28.8 miles
Highlights: Potomac River views, Old Town Alexandria, Dyke Marsh,
    River Farm, Mount Vernon

If George Washington had owned a bicycle, this trail to Mount Vernon might have been completed a lot sooner than it was, in 1973. If you ignore the cars zipping by on the George Washington Memorial Parkway and focus your attention on the river side of the trail, you'll find that the views aren't radically different from those the first president would have seen. The 17-mile trail actually starts at Theodore Roosevelt Island. This tour begins a few miles downriver at the Ronald Reagan National Airport Metro stop.

0.0 Exit the Metro station and follow signs to the bike trail.

Although the trip begins in an airport-industrial milieu, the trail soon breaks out into a plethora of pleasant river views. Approaching Daingerfield Island, you seem to sail into the proverbial "forest of masts."

1.3 Turn left to the Washington Sailing Marina on Daingerfield Island, which is no longer a real island.

This 107-acre park holds an excellent but rather expensive restaurant, Potomawk Landing, plus picnic tables, rest rooms, water

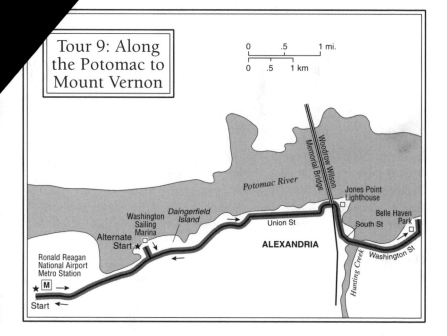

Tour 9: Along the Potomac to Mount Vernon

fountains, phones, and playing fields. There is also a large parking lot, which makes this a good place to begin for people who prefer car starting points to Metro starting points.

2.1 *The trail breaks temporarily in Old Town Alexandria, but signs guide you along city streets. After passing Oronoco Bay Park, a waterfront area with picnic tables, turn left onto Pendleton Street and take an immediate right onto North Union Street.*

3.0 *On your left stands the Torpedo Factory, a World War II munitions operation that now houses craft shops, studios, and galleries.*

Hitch your bike to a street sign and browse, stroll along the waterfront, and walk up King Street (right) for window shopping and information and walking-tour maps at Ramsay House Visitors' Center, 221 King Street. Housed in the home of William Ramsay, a Scottish merchant and city founder, the visitors center can provide information on and directions to other Old Town attractions,

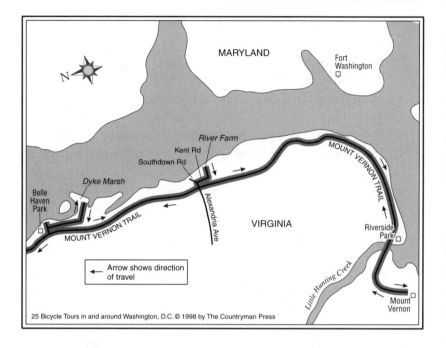

25 Bicycle Tours in and around Washington, D.C. © 1998 by The Countryman Press

including two homes of Robert E. Lee; Christ Church, attended by both Washington and Lee; Gadsby's Tavern, where Washington used to sip Madeira; and the Stabler-Leadbeater Apothecary Shop Museum, where Martha Washington used to buy medicines.

4.0 *At Gibbon and Union Streets, the off-the-road bike trail resumes, leading you through the woods, back along the river, and past an old Ford plant.*

4.3 *Keeping left, along the river and under the Wilson Bridge, you'll see the Jones Point Lighthouse, which warned sailors of nearby sandbars from 1836 to 1925.*

Look along the seawall for the cornerstone that once marked the southernmost corner of the District of Columbia.

Turn right and follow the road directly under the Wilson Bridge to South Street. Turn left.

4.8 *Turn left onto Washington Street, following the marked trail.*

You'll pass some large apartment complexes, cross Hunting Creek, and be treated to a sweeping vista of the wide Potomac.

5.5 *The trail leads through Belle Haven Park, site of an 18th-century settlement of Scottish tobacco merchants.*

Wide green lawns, a marina, picnic tables, and rest rooms are available.

Turn left onto the road that leads to Belle Haven Marina, and then make an immediate right onto a dirt trail that leads through Dyke Marsh.

Dyke Marsh is a wetland sanctuary and the last large tidal freshwater marsh in the Washington area. Except after very heavy rains, the trail is passable for touring bikes. The first encroachment on the marsh's natural state came in the early 1800s, when a settler tried to turn the wetland into farmland by building earthen dikes around it. These were soon abandoned as too costly, and the land reverted to its natural—wet—state. Ride quietly and you may catch glimpses of frogs, turtles, beavers, muskrats, rabbits, shrews, field mice, foxes, and more than 200 species of birds.

6.2 *The Dyke Marsh Trail ends at the river. Reverse direction and return to the main bike trail.*

6.9 *Turn left onto the marina road and left again onto the Mount Vernon Trail.*

7.3 *The trail enters a boardwalk that skirts Dyke Marsh.*

9.1 *The trail exits the woods and enters a small residential enclave.*

Trail signs direct cyclists across a bridge on Alexandria Avenue, but a short detour will allow a visit to River Farm.

Instead of crossing the bridge, continue straight on Southdown Road.

9.2 *Bear right onto Kent Road.*

9.7 *Turn left into River Farm, the headquarters of the American Horticultural Society.*

The house dates from 1757 but was much altered in the 1920s. George Washington bought the property in 1760, gave it its name, and later presented it to his personal secretary, Tobias Lear, as a wedding gift. The house is open for special exhibits. The grounds and beautiful gardens are open summer weekends, and the public is welcome to picnic by the river, under trees that Washington may have planted.

9.9 *After your visit, reverse direction and return to the intersection of Southdown Road and Alexandria Avenue.*

10.7 *Turn left and cross the Alexandria Avenue bridge. Once across, turn left again, following the trail signs.*

The trail stays close to the parkway, skirting some quiet residential neighborhoods, then enters a wooded area and climbs a hill.

12.9 *Rest on a bench and drink in the view of Fort Washington, an early-19th-century bastion on the Maryland shore.*

You'll go up and down a few curvy hills, then cross to the river side of the parkway again.

14.7 *Riverside Park, at the point where Little Hunting Creek empties into the widest point of the river you've glimpsed so far, offers picnic tables as well as views.*

Rest up for some uphill climbs and downhill coasts.

15.8 *Proceed with caution through the large Mount Vernon parking lot to the mansion entrance, probably with a stop at the rest rooms and snack bar first.*

The mansion is open daily including Christmas, and there is an admission fee. In addition to the mansion itself, which contains the bed in which George Washington died, attractions include boxwood gardens, the smokehouse, and the slave burial ground.

Unless you have arranged for someone to pick you up, you'll have to double back along the trail.

27.5 *Arrive at Washington Sailing Marina.*

28.8 *Arrive at Ronald Reagan National Airport Metro station.*

Bicycle Repair Service

Big Wheel Bikes, 2 Prince Street, Alexandria, Virginia (703-739-2300)

Bikes USA, 1506-C Belle View Boulevard, Alexandria, Virginia (703-768-3444)

10
North Arlington Adventure

Location: *Arlington, Virginia*
Terrain: *Moderately hilly*
Road conditions: *Bike trails, park roads, and neighborhood streets with light traffic*
Distance: *7.3 miles*
Highlights: *Donaldson Run Trail, Potomac Overlook Regional Park and Nature Center, Gulf Branch Nature Center with scenic hiking trail to the Potomac River, Walker Chapel, and cemetery*

Arlington, which is actually a county rather than a town or city, is sometimes brushed off as a mere bedroom community for Washington. But it has a character all its own, which has been enlivened in recent years by an influx of refugees from Southeast Asia. An impressive network of bike paths, trails, and parks gives what is really an urban area a countrylike ambience—as do the "runs" or streams that riddle the area, flowing down Arlington's hills and into the Potomac River.

This tour takes the rider through some of Arlington's pleasant older neighborhoods, explores the trail that follows the course of Donaldson Run, visits two wooded parks, and includes an optional walk along Gulf Branch to the Potomac. It also allows visits to two nature centers, including one housed in a former love nest of Pola Negri and Rudolf Valentino.

The trip starts at Arlington's Yorktown High School. To get there from the District, cross Key Bridge and turn right onto Lee Highway, continuing to the intersection with North George Mason Drive. Turn right onto George Mason Drive then make an immediate left onto Florida Street. Florida Street ends at 28th Street, in front of the school parking lot.

0.0 Exit the parking lot and turn left onto 28th Street.

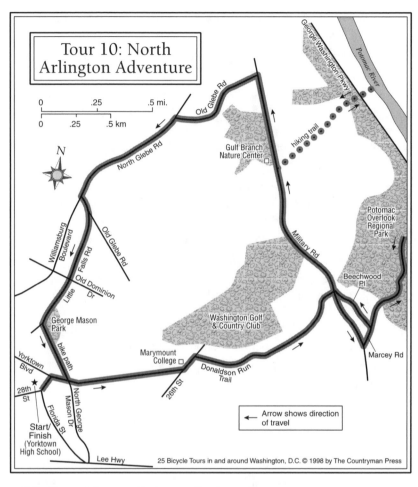

Tour 10: North
Arlington Adventure

0   .25   .5 mi.

0   .25   .5 km

N

0.2 Turn right onto Yorktown Boulevard.

*0.6 After going under an overpass, bear left on 26th Street.
Marymount College will be on your left. Immediately after you
pass the pungent community leaf-mulch pile on your right,
turn right into the woods on the Donaldson Run Trail.*

This mainly downhill trail, which follows the sometimes heavy,
sometimes dry stream, emerges briefly into the surrounding neighborhood to cross North Vermont Street, then reenters the woods.

1.6 The trail ends at Military Road. Turn right and make a brief uphill climb.

1.8 Turn left onto Marcey Road, which will lead you into Potomac Overlook Regional Park.

This is a large park that seems miles away from urban and suburban bustle. It has picnic tables, tennis courts, water fountains, rest rooms, a nature center, and a network of hiking trails.

After riding to the end of the paved road, reverse direction and exit the park.

3.2 Turn right onto Beechwood Place and follow it to the bottom of a hill, where it runs into Military Road. Bear right onto Military Road and bike an up- and downhill course past the Washington Golf and Country Club (left).

4.3 Turn left into Gulf Branch Nature Center.

The stone bungalow that houses the nature center once served as a love nest for Pola Negri and Rudolf Valentino. Lock your bike here and take the hiking trail that follows Gulf Branch down to the Potomac. This beautiful walk will take you under the George Washington Parkway for an unobstructed view of the river.

After leaving the nature center, turn left and continue up Military Road.

4.8 Turn left onto Old Glebe Road.

4.9 On the left is a marker commemorating the site of Fort Ethan Allen.

One of a circle of forts hastily constructed to defend the capital during the Civil War, this fort was supposed to command the approaches to nearby Chain Bridge.

5.1 On the right is the cemetery attached to Walker Chapel.

The earliest grave marks the resting place of David Walker, who died in 1848. The Walker family donated the land for the cemetery and church, which is Methodist. The current structure replaces a frame country church that was built in 1876.

5.1 Old Glebe Road runs into North Glebe Road. Bear left onto North Glebe Road, watching for traffic.

6.3 *Just after North Glebe Road makes a left turn, turn right onto Little Falls Road.*

This road will cross Old Dominion Drive and take you past the Rock Spring United Church of Christ.

6.8 *Just past the church, turn left onto the bike path that leads through George Mason Park.*

7.1 *The bike path ends at the intersection of North George Mason Drive and Yorktown Boulevard. Turn right onto Yorktown Boulevard.*

7.2 *Turn left onto 28th Street.*

7.3 *Enter Yorktown High School parking lot.*

Bicycle Repair Service

The Bicycle Exchange, 3121 Lee Highway, Arlington, Virginia (703-522-1110)

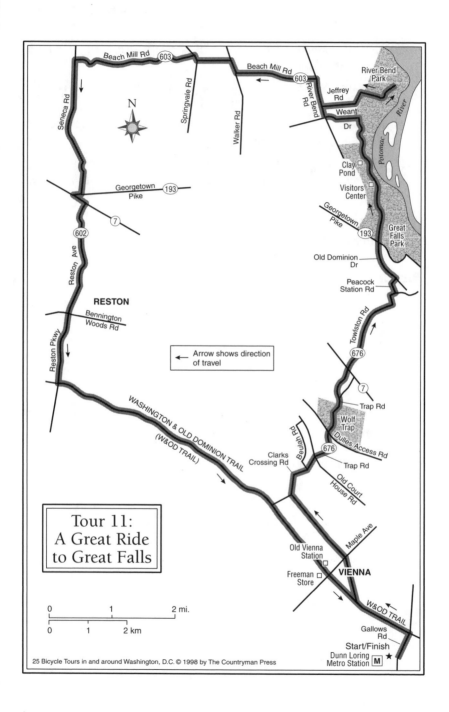

N

Beach Mill Rd (603)

Beach Mill Rd (603)

River Bend Park

Seneca Rd

Springvale Rd

Walker Rd

River Bend Rd

Jeffrey Rd

Weant Dr

Potomac River

Georgetown Pike (193)

(7)

(602)

Reston Ave

Clay Pond

Visitors Center

Georgetown Pike (193)

Great Falls Park

Old Dominion Dr

Peacock Station Rd

RESTON

Bennington Woods Rd

Reston Pkwy

Towlston Rd

(676)

(7)

Trap Rd

Wolf Trap

Dulles Access Rd

(676)

Trap Rd

Arrow shows direction of travel

WASHINGTON & OLD DOMINION TRAIL

(W&OD TRAIL)

Beulah Rd

Clarks Crossing Rd

Old Court House Rd

Maple Ave

Tour 11:
A Great Ride
to Great Falls

Old Vienna Station

Freeman Store

VIENNA

W&OD TRAIL

| 0 | 1 | 2 mi. |
| 0 | 1 | 2 km |

Gallows Rd

Start/Finish
Dunn Loring
Metro Station M ★

25 Bicycle Tours in and around Washington, D.C. © 1998 by The Countryman Press

11
A Great Ride to Great Falls

Location: Northern Virginia
Metro access: Dunn Loring
Terrain: Hilly
Road conditions: Paved trail and roads with mainly light traffic
Distance: 36 miles
Highlights: The Great Falls of the Potomac, Riverbend Park, Reston, Vienna, the Washington and Old Dominion Trail

On its way to the sea from the mountains of West Virginia, the Potomac River really picks up speed as it approaches Washington—dropping 80 feet in less than a mile and roaring through Mather Gorge in a rush of churning white water. This point on the river, known as Great Falls, has long attracted visitors, who come to gaze at the raw power of nature, to picnic, fish, hike, rock climb, or even boat in the white water below the falls. At the turn of the century, the Washington and Old Dominion Railroad built a branch line to carry excursionists to the falls, where an inn, a dance pavilion, and a carousel added to the natural attractions. Today the railroad, the inn, the pavilion, and the carousel are gone, but the park is still so popular that the parking lot is sometimes full—and closed to visitors—by noon.

You can avoid Great Falls gridlock by cycling to the falls, on a route that takes advantage of the Washington and Old Dominion Trail—the roadbed of the main line of the railroad to Great Falls—and travels for a short distance on Old Dominion Drive, the roadbed of the spur to Great Falls. After a visit to Riverbend Park, a quieter spot on the Potomac upstream from the falls, the tour continues through the hills of northern Virginia, runs through the pioneer planned community of Reston, and rejoins the W&OD Trail for a visit to Vienna, a town that has honored its railroad past by restoring a caboose, which stands adjacent to the trail.

Appropriately enough, this tour begins at a Metrorail stop, the Dunn Loring station, which affords easy access to the W&OD Trail.

0.0 *Exit the Dunn Loring station, turning left onto Gallows Road. There is a paved trail along the road.*

0.7 *Turn left onto the W&OD Trail.*

Although it traverses a suburban area, the trail is pleasantly wooded. Watch for wild Turk's-cap lilies, which burst into blossom in July.

2.0 *A historical marker indicates the spot where the railroad was used during the Civil War to carry a South Carolina regiment to a battle with Ohio volunteers.*

3.1 *The trail crosses Maple Avenue.*

Restaurants and food stores are available on this street, the main thoroughfare of Vienna.

Cross Maple at the stoplight and continue on the trail.

4.9 *Exit the trail to the right through the small parking lot that lies across the trail from the Clarks Crossing soccer field and park. Proceed along Clarks Crossing Road.*

5.7 *Clarks Crossing Road stops at Beulah Road. Turn left onto Beulah Road.*

5.8 *At the stop sign, Beulah Road turns left. Cross Old Court House Road and continue straight on Trap Road (VA 676).*

6.4 *At the stop sign, follow Trap Road to the left.*

You'll pass the Barns at Wolf Trap, part of the Filene Center for the Performing Arts, which is administered by the National Park Service.

6.2 *After crossing over the Dulles Access Road on a bridge, Trap Road passes the main part of Wolf Trap Farm Park.*

The location of a popular outdoor summer theater, the park was once the farm of Mrs. Jouett Shouse, who donated it to the nation.

7.7 *Trap Road turns right. Follow Towlston Road, which continues straight ahead as VA 676.*

8.2 *Towlston Road crosses VA 7 and winds through an area of*

With a mighty roar, the Potomac River careens down
the fall line at Great Falls, Virginia.

large homes set back from the road.

8.6 *Turn left onto Peacock Station Road.*

8.9 *Peacock Station Road ends. Turn left onto Old Dominion Drive,
following the route the railroad to Great Falls used to take.*

10.6 *Old Dominion Drive crosses Georgetown Pike and continues
down a hill and through the woods into Great Falls Park.*

11.5 *Stop at the tollbooth to pay a 50-cent-per-bicycle admission
fee and to pick up a trail map before proceeding straight
ahead to the visitors center.*

The visitors center has exhibits on the geology and history of the area, plus rest rooms, a snack bar, and a bookstore. Lock your bike at the rack outside the visitors center and walk to the overlook for a spectacular view of the falls. Look downstream for kayakers daring the white water. Near the observation platforms are ruins of some of the workings on the Patowmack Canal, a pet project of George Washington. Construction on this Great Falls bypass began in 1786 and was completed two years after Washington died—giving reality to his frequent toast: "Success to the navigation of the Potomac!" Unfortunately, the high cost of building his canal eventually bankrupted the company, and the route was abandoned in 1830, leaving the way open for the Chesapeake and Ohio Canal on the Maryland side of the river. (See Tour 7.)

After leaving the visitors center, continue to the end of the parking lot. On your left, you will see Clay Pond.

11.7 *Turn left onto the paved fire road at the head of Clay Pond.*

It soon turns to easily negotiable dirt and gravel and winds uphill through the woods.

12.7 *The trail ends at Weant Drive. Turn left and be prepared for a series of roller-coaster hills.*

13.3 *Turn right onto River Bend Road (VA 603).*

13.5 *Turn right onto Jeffery Road, which makes a left and then turns right into River Bend Park.*

14.3 *Proceed past the tollgate (no fee for bikes) to the visitors center.*

The visitors center has a snack bar and picnic tables on a deck that overlooks a sweeping lawn leading down to the Potomac.

After seeing the fury of Great Falls, you may find it hard to believe that this is the same river only a mile or so upstream. It's quite tranquil here, with boats for rent and a nature center.

After a respite in this pretty and peaceful park, double back on Jeffery Road, riding through the park gates to the intersection with River Bend Road.

16.3 *Turn right onto River Bend Road.*

16.8 *River Bend Road ends. Turn left onto Beach Mill Road, the continuation of VA 603.*

18.3 Beach Mill Road seems to end, but really doesn't. Turn right onto Walker Road.

18.4 Turn left and pick up Beach Mill Road again. This is an area of large homes and horse farms.

19.0 At the intersection with Springvale Road stands the Auberge Chez François, a very popular French-style country inn, successor to a downtown restaurant.

In Sally Quinn's Washington novel, *Regrets Only*, the wife of the vice president begins her illicit relationship with a journalist here, after being smuggled out of the vice presidential mansion in a garbage can. The restaurant is surrounded by a large garden where some of the herbs used in the kitchen are grown. In off-peak hours, you can sometimes see the help eating outside the kitchen door, a vignette out of a French painting. The restaurant is open for dinner only, but begins serving Sundays at 2 PM. Jackets and ties are required for men.

19.0 Continue across Springvale Road on Beach Mill Road, which enters a very hilly phase, winding past expensive-looking, brand-new "châteaux."

21.2 Beach Mill Road ends. Turn left onto Seneca Road (VA 602).

Look to your right for spectacular views of distant blue mountains.

23.3 Seneca Road ends at Georgetown Pike (VA 193). Follow Georgetown Pike to the right for about a hundred feet, then cross VA 7 at the light. Turn left onto VA 7, riding on the shoulder to the frontage road.

23.5 Turn right onto Reston Avenue, the continuation of VA 602.

There is a food store at the intersection. When it enters the thriving "new town" of Reston, Reston Avenue becomes Reston Parkway. Laid out in 1892 by Dr. Carl Adolph Max Wiehle, who acquired a 7,200-acre tract here with a partner, the town did not become a reality until the early 1960s.

25.3 At the intersection with Bennington Woods Road, a paved bike path begins, running parallel to Reston Parkway.

It continues, with a few interruptions, to the intersection of Reston Parkway and the W&OD Trail.

26.5 *Turn left onto the W&OD Trail, which runs through fields and over lowlands crisscrossed by small streams.*

Listen for frogs and watch for river otters and herons. A stone-arch bridge carries the trail over Piney Branch.

32.7 *On your left is the old Vienna railroad station, which is currently leased to the Northern Virginia Model Railroaders Association.*

These hobbyists are in the process of modeling a section of the Western North Carolina Railroad, complete with operating trains, scenery, and buildings. Several times a year the railroaders hold an open house at the old station to show visitors their work in progress (call 703-938-5157 for dates and information). On the other side of the trail stands a bright red refurbished caboose, which the town of Vienna acquired after Virginia repealed the law requiring manned cabooses on trains.

32.8 *On your right, at the corner of Church Street and the trail, stands the Freeman Store.*

This emporium dates to 1859 and is now operated as a general store by Historic Vienna, Inc. It's open Sundays from noon to 5 PM and sells crafts, handmade items, and penny candy. The house also served as the town's post office and as its first railroad station. During the Civil War, the building was occupied by both Northern and Southern troops as the village, with its strategically important railroad, changed hands frequently.

32.9 *The trail crosses Maple Avenue, Vienna's main artery.*

The town, settled in the 1760s by Scots and originally called Ayr Hill, was rechristened Vienna in 1858 by a doctor who had lived in Vienna, New York, and studied medicine in Vienna, Austria. Although part of the mushrooming Washington suburban area, Vienna retains its small-town charm.

35.3 *Turn right onto Gallows Road.*

36.0 *Turn right into the Dunn Loring Metro station.*

Bicycle Repair Service

Nova Cycle, 124 Maple Avenue W, Vienna, Virginia (703-938-7191)

12
A Virginia Triangle

Location: *Arlington and Alexandria, Virginia*
Terrain: *Gradual uphill climbs at the start, then downhill or flat*
Road conditions: *Paved off-road bike trails with a few "portages" on suburban streets*
Distance: *16.2 miles*
Highlights: *Bluemont Park, Four Mile Run, the new Ronald Reagan National Airport terminal, views of the Washington Monument, Lincoln Memorial, Kennedy Center*

The great thing about the proliferation of bike trails in the Washington area is that you can mix and match them, creating tours that require only short stints on city and suburban streets. This triangle-shaped tour uses parts of four bike trails: the I-66/Custis Trail, the Bluemont Junction Trail, the Four Mile Run Trail, and the Mount Vernon Trail. After a gradual climb at the outset, the tour glides downhill, following Four Mile Run as it changes from a tree-shaded babbling brook to a broad tidal creek. The last few miles follow the Potomac River upstream, with spectacular views of Washington at every turn.

The tour begins in the parking lot for Theodore Roosevelt Island, accessible from the northbound lanes of the George Washington Parkway. The nearest Metro stop is Arlington Cemetery. Or, from the District, you can ride your bike across Memorial Bridge and take the Mount Vernon Trail north to Roosevelt Island.

0.0 *Exit the Roosevelt Island parking lot and follow the I-66/Custis Trail up a ramp and through busy Rosslyn.*

The paved trail winds uphill through commercial strips and residential neighborhoods.

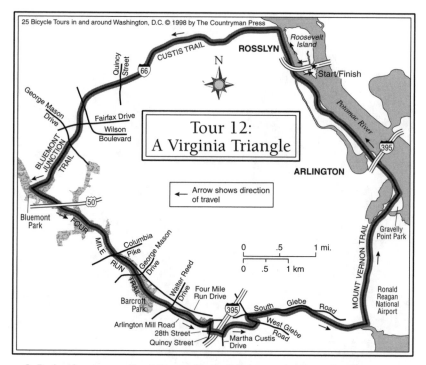

25 Bicycle Tours in and around Washington, D.C. © 1998 by The Countryman Press

Tour 12:
A Virginia Triangle

ROSSLYN

Roosevelt Island

Start/Finish

CUSTIS TRAIL

N

Quincy Street

66

George Mason Drive

Fairfax Drive

Wilson Boulevard

BLUEMONT JUNCTION TRAIL

ARLINGTON

Potomac River

395

Arrow shows direction of travel

50

Bluemont Park

FOUR MILE RUN TRAIL

Columbia Pike

George Mason Drive

Walter Reed Drive

Four Mile Run Drive

Barcroft Park

Arlington Mill Road

28th Street

Quincy Street

Martha Custis Drive

395

South Glebe Road

West Glebe Road

Road

MOUNT VERNON TRAIL

Gravelly Point Park

Ronald Reagan National Airport

0   .5   1 mi.

0   .5   1 km

3.5 At the crest of a hill, turn left, following the sign for the Bluemont Junction Trail.

If you come to George Mason Drive, you have missed the turnoff, so go back. This spur will take you downhill to the sidewalk along busy Fairfax Drive in the Ballston section of Arlington. Ballston is a good place to find food.

3.6 Cross Fairfax Drive in the crosswalk that leads to the Holiday Inn. Turn right, doubling back on the opposite side of the street. Then take the first left onto the Bluemont Junction Trail, which goes through a small park.

3.7 Where the park ends, cross both George Mason Drive and Wilson Boulevard and pick up the trail to your right.

Continue through wooded and meadowlike parkland bordered by the backyards of diverse Arlington, sharing the trail with families pushing strollers and shepherding kids on training wheels.

The Mount Vernon Trail hugs the Potomac shoreline,
affording views across the river to Washington.

4.6 *The trail crosses Four Mile Run Drive and runs into a large athletic field.*

This is the junction with the Four Mile Run Trail.

Turn left and continue through beautiful Bluemont Park.

4.9 *Here you will find clean, modern rest rooms.*

The trail follows the stream through woods and alongside gardens. Watch for garter snakes on the trail.

6.2 *The trail crosses Columbia Pike.*

A few yards to your left before crossing the Pike is the Town Express Carryout, with Asian, Spanish and American food. Try the Vietnamese summer rolls.

6.7 *Turn right onto George Mason Drive and cross the bridge that goes over Four Mile Run.*

6.8 *Turn left onto the trail through Barcroft Park, a lovely wooded area with picnic tables.*

7.7 *Emerge from Barcroft Park and continue on the trail to your left. Cross Walter Reed Drive at the light.*

8.4 *At the trail sign, cross Arlington Mill Drive on your left and continue one block on Quincy Street through the booming Shirlington area, which offers many restaurants. Turn left onto 28th Street and then make an immediate left onto the over-pass that will take you to the other side of I-395.*

8.8 *At the other side of the overpass, turn left onto Martha Custis Drive, a low-traffic residential street through a suburban neighborhood.*

9.3 *Martha Custis Drive dead-ends on West Glebe Road. Go left onto the sidewalk along West Glebe Road.*

9.5 *At the busy intersection of West Glebe Road, Four Mile Run Drive, and South Glebe Road, cross West Glebe Road to the right and follow the trail, which runs between Four Mile Run—the stream—and South Glebe Road.*

You will traverse small parks and ride along the backs of garden apartments. Watch Four Mile Run grow broader and become a habitat for waterfowl, a sure sign that the Potomac is coming up.

11.6 *After passing a water treatment plant with educational signs explaining its operation and going under several low bridges, look to your right to see Four Mile Run flow into the Potomac River. Round a curve and join the Mount Vernon Trail at Ronald Reagan National Airport. Head north in the direction of Washington, D.C.*

12.6 *Look to your right for a view of the glitzy new $450 million Ronald Reagan National Airport terminal. Follow the trail through Gravelly Point Park, a popular picnic spot, and continue along the Potomac.*

Across the river, you'll see the Washington, Jefferson, and Lincoln Memorials and the Kennedy Center.

16.2 *Return to the Roosevelt Island parking lot.*

Bicycle Repair Service

Metropolis Bicycles, 4056 So. 28th Street, Arlington, Virginia (703-671-1700)

13
Cycling the Thirties

Location: *Prince George's County, Maryland*
Metro access: *Greenbelt*
Terrain: *Moderately hilly in the Beltsville Agriculture Research Center; almost flat in Greenbelt*
Road conditions: *On-road bicycle trail and light-traffic roads*
Distance: *14.4 miles*
Highlights: *Country roads in the Beltsville Agricultural Research Center; the planned New Deal town of Greenbelt, with its art moderne architecture*

One day in the '30s, brain-truster G. Rexford Tugwell took President Franklin Delano Roosevelt for a ride in the country around Washington. He showed him a site adjacent to the Agricultural Research Center at Beltsville and proposed that a "garden community" be built there for low- and middle-income families, so that they could live in a "green belt" convenient to but apart from cities. Greenbelt, Maryland, was one of three such places built in the United States, and it is still a thriving community, though no longer under federal control.

This tour starts at the Greenbelt Metro station, follows a well-marked bike trail to the town, and visits both the adjacent Agricultural Research Center and historic Greenbelt, with a stop at the museum.

0.0 From the Metro station, proceed through the parking lot toward the exit on Cherrywood Lane.

0.4 Turn left onto Cherrywood Lane.

0.6 Cross Cherrywood Lane in the crosswalk. Turn left and cross the bridge over the Capital Beltway.

0.9 Turn right onto Ivy Lane, which has a marked bike lane and

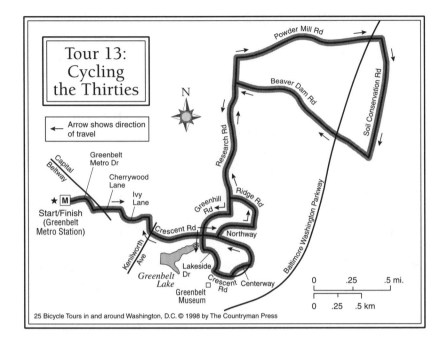

Tour 13:
Cycling
the Thirties

N

← Arrow shows direction
  of travel

Greenbelt
Metro Dr

Cherrywood
Lane

Ivy
Lane

Capital Beltway

★ M

Start/Finish
(Greenbelt
Metro Station)

Kenilworth Ave

Greenhill Rd

Crescent Rd

Northway

Ridge Rd

Research Rd

Powder Mill Rd

Beaver Dam Rd

Soil Conservation Rd

Baltimore Washington Parkway

Lakeside Dr

Greenbelt Lake

Crescent Rd

Centerway

Greenbelt
Museum

0   .25   .5 mi.

0   .25   .5 km

25 Bicycle Tours in and around Washington, D.C. © 1998 by The Countryman Press

leads through an industrial park.

1.2 Where the bike lane ends, turn right, following Greenbelt's Cross City bicycle route signs.

1.4 Cross Kenilworth Avenue at the light and continue on Crescent Road, which has a path alongside the road.

2.3 At St. Hugh's Church, turn left onto Northway.

2.7 Turn left onto Ridge Road.

3.2 Turn right onto Research Road, ignoring the GATE CLOSED sign, which does not apply to cyclists.

The road leads to the U.S. Agricultural Research Center, more than 7,000 acres of woods and farmland used for researching methods to improve agriculture. The plump-breasted Beltsville turkey was developed here. The buildings and grounds are off-limits to the public, but the roads are open. Some of them are closed to automobile traffic on weekends, making for very pleasant cycling in a rural environment.

3.4 If the gate is closed, slide your bike under it and continue down a long hill.

4.3 Slide your bike under another gate and cross Beaver Dam Road. Continue on Research Road, which is lined with fields on one side, woods on the other.

4.6 Turn right onto Powder Mill Road, which carries automobile traffic but has a marked bike lane.

4.7 At the top of a hill, on your right, is a log lodge built by the Civilian Conservation Corps in 1936–1937.

The lodge serves as a visitors center, but is open only on weekdays.

6.0 Powder Mill Road crosses under the Baltimore Washington Parkway.

6.3 Turn right onto Soil Conservation Road.

6.7 Stop to admire the pigs lounging in the sun on your left.

7.5 Turn right onto Beaver Dam Road, which winds downhill through oak and pine woods.

9.3 Turn left onto Research Road, sliding your bike under the gate.

9.6 Stop and look to your left at the beaver dam. Then climb the hill you descended before.

10.2 Exit the Agricultural Research Center and continue on Research Road, crossing Ridge Road.

10.6 Turn right onto Greenhill Road, which curves downhill.

11.0 Cross Crescent Road and continue on a gravel path that leads to Greenbelt Lake. Cross over the end of the lake on a footbridge and continue up a path between houses.

11.2 Turn left onto Lakeside Drive.

11.5 Turn left onto Crescent.

11.7 Stop at 10-B Crescent Road (right) for the Greenbelt Museum, open Sunday 1–5 or by arrangement (301-474-1936).

The museum (admission free but donations accepted) is actually one of the original homes, built in 1937. At that time, the two-story house rented for $31 a month. Competition for the homes was stiff, and renters faced stringent rules. Wives had to agree to stay at home, and no laundry could be hung out on Sundays. The museum is furnished with the original 1930s appliances and "moderne" furniture from Scandinavia, which residents were encouraged to purchase in the local cooperative. Many of the museum docents are longtime residents of Greenbelt, and give very informative tours.

On your left stands the old Greenbelt Elementary School, now the community center. The relief sculptures on the front of the building illustrate the preamble to the Constitution. They were commissioned by the WPA and executed by sculptor Lenore Thomas.

Turn left into Centerway, entering the '30s-style shopping center with its co-op, credit union, and art moderne movie theater.

The centerpiece of the small mall is another Lenore Thomas sculpture entitled *Mother and Child.*

11.9 *Exit the shopping center and turn left, continuing on Crescent Road.*

13.1 *Cross Kenilworth Avenue at the light and follow the bicycle path.*

13.3 *Turn left onto Ivy Lane.*

13.6 *Turn left onto Cherrywood Lane, taking the bike lane across the bridge.*

14.4 *Enter the Greenbelt Metro station parking lot.*

Bicycle Repair Service

College Park Bicycles, 4360 Knox Road, College Park, Maryland (301-864-2211)

14
Taking Off on the Indian Creek Trail

Location: Prince George's County, Maryland
Metro access: College Park
Terrain: Flat
Road conditions: A paved trail and light-traffic roads with sidewalks
Distance: 5.3 miles
Highlights: Indian Creek Trail, Lake Artemesia, the 94th Aero Squadron restaurant, historic College Park Airport

Though more an excuse for a weekend brunch than a rigorous ride, this tour has just about everything—but in small quantities: a pleasant trail, a pretty lake, a historic site with a museum, and a relaxing restaurant. It makes a great family outing.

The tour begins at the College Park stop on Metro's Green Line, at Paint Branch Parkway and River Road. (Parking is free on weekends.) It follows a designated on-sidewalk bike path along River Road to Riverdale Park, where it picks up the Indian Creek Hiker-Biker Trail (also known as the Northeast Branch Trail). That trail winds through woods along Indian Creek and Paint Branch, parts of the northeast branch of the Anacostia River. The tour diverges from the trail for some Zen biking around lovely Lake Artemesia: Pause to admire the view from the gazebos and boardwalks that dot the artificial lake. It then loops back along the trail, skirting the runways of College Park Airport. Stop for brunch at the 94th Aero Squadron restaurant before visiting the historic little airport and its museum and returning to the starting point.

0.0 Exit the parking lot of the College Park Metro station and turn right onto River Road, which has a sidewalk.

0.8 Turn right onto Haig Drive into Riverdale Community Park.

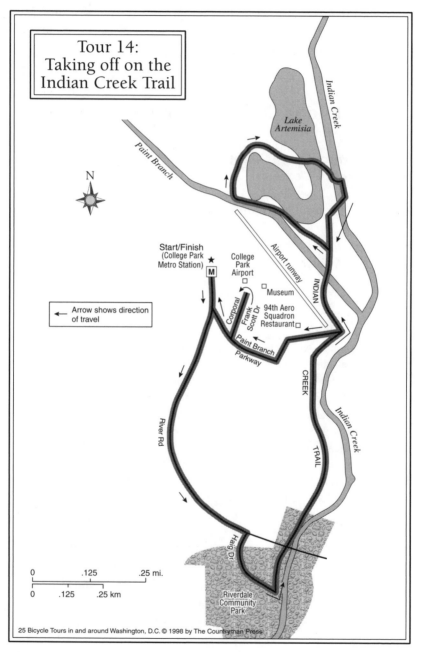

Tour 14:
Taking off on the
Indian Creek Trail

Lake
Artemisia

Paint Branch

Indian Creek

N

Airport runway

Start/Finish
(College Park
Metro Station)

College
Park
Airport

INDIAN

☐ Museum

Arrow shows direction
of travel

Corporal

Frank
Scott Dr

94th Aero
Squadron
Restaurant ☐

Paint Branch
Parkway

CREEK

River Rd

Indian Creek

TRAIL

Haig Dr

0   .125   .25 mi.

0   .125   .25 km

Riverdale
Community
Park

25 Bicycle Tours in and around Washington, D.C. © 1998 by The Countryman Press

1.1 Turn left onto the Indian Creek Trail (also known as the Northeast Branch Trail), which leads under a bridge and along the stream, through well-groomed parkland.

1.8 The trail goes under Paint Branch Parkway and along the runways of College Park Airport.

This is a good spot to take a break and watch the Cessnas take off and land. The trail then crosses crystalline Paint Branch.

2.7 Turn left, off the trail, into a small park centered on Lake Artemesia. Bear left around the ornamental lake, which was created by Metro to obtain fill to raise the track bed on a nearby section of Metrorail.

There are lakeside gazebos, rest rooms, docks for sunbathing, and an observation platform for wildlife-watching. According to newspaper reports, Metro actually saved money by digging here rather than hauling the dirt from elsewhere. About two-thirds of the way around the lake, signs will ask you to dismount and walk your bike.

3.8 Rejoin the trail, turning right. After passing the airport runways again, you will see the 94th Aero Squadron restaurant on your right.

4.3 Take the dirt path off the trail and into the restaurant parking lot.

The restaurant masquerades as a French farmhouse converted to a U.S. Army air post during World War I. An old ambulance graces the courtyard and the decor is heavy on war-bond posters and similar memorabilia. Rest rooms are called latrines. The view takes in the airport runways.

After brunch, exit the parking lot onto Paint Branch Parkway, which has a sidewalk.

4.8 Turn right onto Corporal Frank Scott Drive, which goes through a mini-industrial park to the airport.

5.0 Turn right to the museum, housed temporarily in a trailer.

The museum is free, though donations are accepted. It's open weekends from 11 to 5 and Wednesday through Friday from 11 to 3. It includes great old photographs and other artifacts of the

The 94th Aero Squadron restaurant, overlooking the runways of historic College Park Airport, carries out its fighter pilot motif with checkpoints, bunkers, even "latrines."

world's oldest continually operated airport, opened in 1909 when the Wright brothers brought their plane here to teach Army officers to fly. In 1912, military pilot "Hap" Arnold made the first mile-high flight from here.

After visiting the airport and museum, reverse direction on Corporal Frank Scott Drive.

5.2 *Turn right onto Paint Branch Parkway and then right onto River Road.*

5.3 *Return to the College Park metro station parking lot.*

Bicycle repair service

Riverdale Cycle and Fitness, 4503 Queensbury Road, Riverdale, Maryland (301-864-4731)

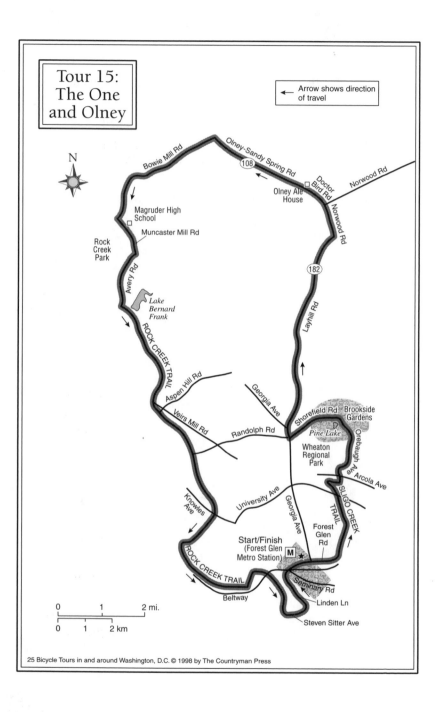

Tour 15:
The One
and Olney

Arrow shows direction
of travel

N

Bowie Mill Rd

Olney-Sandy Spring Rd

108

Olney Ale
House

Doctor
Bird Rd

Norwood Rd

Magruder High
School

Muncaster Mill Rd

Norwood Rd

Rock
Creek
Park

Avery Rd

182

Lake
Bernard
Frank

ROCK CREEK TRAIL

Layhill Rd

Aspen Hill Rd

Veirs Mill Rd

Georgia Ave

Randolph Rd

Shorefield Rd

Brookside
Gardens

Pine Lake

Wheaton
Regional
Park

Orebaugh Av

Arcola Ave

Knowles Ave

University Ave

Georgia Ave

SLIGO CREEK TRAIL

Start/Finish
(Forest Glen
Metro Station)

M

Forest
Glen
Rd

ROCK CREEK TRAIL

Beltway

Seminary Rd

Linden Ln

Steven Sitter Ave

0   1   2 mi.

0   1   2 km

25 Bicycle Tours in and around Washington, D.C. © 1998 by The Countryman Press

15
The One and Olney

Location: *Montgomery County, Maryland*
Metro access: *Forest Glen*
Terrain: *Hilly on roads, almost flat on bike trails*
Road conditions: *Some busy streets, most with sidewalks, bike lanes, or shoulders; three off-road trails, short stretches of dirt and gravel paths*
Distance: *33.2 miles*
Highlights: *Sligo Creek Trail, Brookside Gardens, the Olney Ale House, Rock Creek Park, Forest Glen Annex*

This tour uses two of metropolitan Washington's vertical greenbelts—Sligo Creek Park and Rock Creek Park—to escort you away from suburban sprawl and into a countrylike setting. Although getting there is half the fun, the destination is also very attractive: the cozy, funky Olney Ale House, host to travelers since 1924. The tour begins and ends at the Forest Glen Metro station of the Red Line, just outside the Beltway on Georgia Avenue.

0.0 *Exit the Forest Glen Metro station and turn left onto Forest Glen Road, crossing busy Georgia Avenue at the light.*

0.7 *Turn left onto the Sligo Creek Trail. This multiuse paved trail runs on both sides of shady, sylvan Sligo Creek.*

2.3 *Cross University Avenue and continue on the trail, to your right.*

3.0 *The trail bears left, but this tour goes straight, on Orebaugh Avenue, following signs to the Wheaton Regional Park athletic complex.*

The Olney Ale House, which has been offering food and drink to travelers
since 1924, accommodates cyclists either inside or on the patio.

3.2 *Cross Arcola Avenue and continue straight, following the road into Wheaton Regional Park, past tennis courts and a skating rink. Bear left after the skating rink onto a dirt-and-gravel road that leads past pretty Pine Lake.*

Just past Pine Lake, to your right, lies Brookside Gardens. No bikes are allowed in the gardens, but you can lock your bike to the fence and walk through. The 50-acre facility includes a tropical conservatory, a Japanese garden with teahouse, an azalea walk, a rose garden, and an aquatic garden.

After your visit, continue on the paved trail, bearing right, up a hill.

4.3 *Rest rooms are available near the playground. Continue straight past the rest rooms to the park exit.*

4.5 *Turn right onto Shorefield Road.*

4.8 *Turn right onto busy Georgia Avenue, riding on the sidewalk.*

5.2 *At a busy intersection, bear right onto Layhill Road (MD 182).*

This moderately hilly road has a bike lane. It winds through a suburban area and gradually becomes more rural.

10.2 *At the light in front of a liquor store (cold sodas available), turn left, with MD 182, onto Norwood Road.*

11.1 *Norwood Road turns right, but continue straight on MD 182, which becomes Doctor Bird Road.*

12.0 *At the intersection of Doctor Bird Road and Olney–Sandy Spring Road (MD 108) stands the Olney Ale House (right), a good destination for rest and refreshments.*

This establishment was founded as The Corner Cupboard in 1924 and has offered food and drink to travelers ever since. It also serves patrons of the Olney Theater, a repertory and summer theater, across the road. It's so popular with cyclists that there's a bike rack. Seating is available either inside the pleasant sprawling house or outdoors.

After your stop, turn left in front of the inn and cross Doctor Bird Road at the light. Then head north on the off-road 108 trail, which runs alongside MD 108.

14.3 *Turn left on Bowie Mill Road, which winds up and down hills.*

17.6 *At the light, turn left onto Muncaster Mill Road, which passes Magruder High School.*

18.6 *Turn right onto Avery Road, following signs to Rock Creek Regional Park. Ignore the two entrances to the park and stay on Avery Road.*

20.2 *Just past the entrance to Lake Bernard Frank, at the bottom of a wooded hill, turn left onto the Rock Creek Trail.*

Follow this paved and shaded trail through the park. The trail clings close to the creek as it gurgles its way from the Montgomery County hills over rocks and boulders to its mouth on the Potomac in Washington. There are lots of green glades and nature-made beaches if you want to rest or wade.

22.9 *Go through the parking lot and follow Aspen Hill Road to the intersection with Viers Mill Road. Cross Viers Mill Road at the light and continue on the trail.*

24.8 *Cross Randolph Road and continue on the trail.*

26.7 *At the intersection with Knowles Avenue, you can turn left and take an optional side trip to the Howard Avenue antiques district of Kensington.*

This will add 1.4 miles to the trip.

30.7 *Almost directly in front of you looms the Mormon Temple.*

The exuberant, soaring white-marble structure is topped by a gilded trumpeting angel, Moroni. Mormons believe that Moroni lived in America in the fourth century A.D. and compiled the Book of Mormon. It was Moroni who appeared to Joseph Smith in 1827 and instructed him to found the Church of Jesus Christ of Latter-Day Saints. The temple was completed in 1974.

31.3 *Just past the temple, take the side trail to the left marked* FOREST GLEN METRO.

You will go through woods and up a hill and emerge on Steven Sitter Avenue in the Forest Glen Annex of Walter Reed Army Medical Center.

Turn left onto Steven Sitter Road and follow it to the intersection with Linden Lane. Turn left onto Linden Lane.

The annex, once a resort, in 1924 became a girls finishing school, the National Park Seminary. On the right side of Linden Lane stands a shingled frame pagoda, formerly a sorority house.

Follow Linden Lane down the hill, out of the Annex and across the Beltway.

32.3 *After crossing both the railroad tracks and Seminary Road, turn right onto Forest Glen Road.*

33.2 *Turn left into Forest Glen Metro station.*

Bicycle Repair Service

The Bicycle Place, 13605 Connecticut Avenue, Aspen Hill, Maryland (301-460-0420)

Griffin Cycle Inc., 18050 Georgia Avenue, Olney, Maryland (301-774-3970)

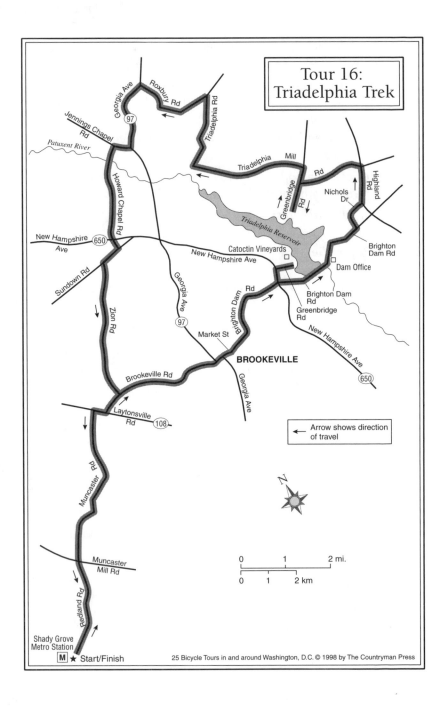

Tour 16:
Triadelphia Trek

Georgia Ave
Roxbury Rd
Triadelphia Rd
97
Jennings Chapel Rd
Patuxent River
Triadelphia   Mill   Rd
Highland Rd
Howard Chapel Rd
Greenbridge Rd
Nichols Dr
Triadelphia Reservoir
New Hampshire Ave
650
Catoctin Vineyards
New Hampshire Ave
Brighton Dam Rd
Sundown Rd
Dam Office
Zion Rd
Georgia Ave
Brighton Dam   Rd
Brighton Dam Rd
Greenbridge Rd
97
Brighton Dam Rd
Market St
New Hampshire Ave
BROOKEVILLE
650
Brookeville Rd
Georgia Ave
Laytonsville Rd
108

← Arrow shows direction of travel

N

Muncaster Rd

Muncaster Mill Rd

0   1   2 mi.
0   1   2 km

Redland Rd

Shady Grove
Metro Station
Ⓜ ★ Start/Finish

25 Bicycle Tours in and around Washington, D.C. © 1998 by The Countryman Press

16
Triadelphia Trek

Location: *Montgomery and Howard Counties in Maryland*
Metro access: *Shady Grove*
Terrain: *Moderately hilly to hilly*
Road conditions: *Mostly light traffic, some short rides on roads with heavy traffic; paved roads and some optional dirt roads*
Distance: *44 miles*
Highlights: *Historic Brookeville, Catoctin Vineyards, Triadelphia Reservoir, Brighton Dam*

Brighton Dam blocks the Patuxent River to create Triadelphia Reservoir, a major source of water for 1.3 million people in Montgomery and Prince George's Counties. The Triadelphia watershed area also provides superb recreation and scenery. It's a mecca for fishermen, and affords good picnic spots and places for people who want to get away from the hustle and bustle of the metropolis. There are no bike trails and there is no road that hugs the shoreline, but it's possible to ride across the dam and around the reservoir on low-traffic roads with side trips for rests, picnics, and views of the water.

The trip starts at the Shady Grove station, about as far into the country as Metro will take you. In a short time after exiting the Metro station, you'll be in the country—although you'll never be far from encroaching development. Country roads will lead you through wooded areas, past small farms and babbling brooks to lovely, leafy Brookeville, a 19th-century town where people sit on wide front porches and watch the passing parade.

After a stop at Catoctin Vineyards, the closest winery to Washington, you'll be at the reservoir's edge. Please remember that swimming and wading are prohibited. (If you must wade, there's an inviting stretch of the Patuxent farther on.) Also remember that bike helmets are required by law for children 16 and under in both Howard and Montgomery Counties.

0.0 *Exit the Shady Grove Metro station by the bus route and turn left onto Redland Road.*

2.8 *Cross Muncaster Mill Road.*

You'll find fast food, shops, and gas stations. Redlands Road continues as Muncaster Road.

6.7 *Muncaster Road ends. Turn right onto Laytonsville Road (MD 108).*

George's Liquor Store (right) has carryout food.

6.8 *Taking care to avoid the traffic on Laytonsville Road, turn left onto Brookeville Road.*

This is a pleasant, three-mile stretch past farms and woods.

9.8 *Brookeville Road ends at Georgia Avenue (MD 97).*

Bear right onto Georgia Avenue and follow it as it winds up a hill, past grand but unpretentious houses into the town of Brookeville.

10.0 *At the top of the hill stands the post office (right).*

After the British burned the White House, James and Dolley Madison found refuge near here on August 26, 1814, in the home of Brookeville postmaster Caleb Bentley.

10.0 *Georgia Avenue turns right in front of the post office.*

The tour goes straight, past the side of the post office, on Market Street. Market Street takes you past more lovely homes. At the bottom of a hill, it leaves town and becomes Brighton Dam Road, which rolls up and down hills.

12.7 *Turn left onto New Hampshire Avenue (MD 650).*

This is not a major artery at this point, but watch for traffic.

13.1 *Turn right onto Greenbridge Road.*

Watch immediately on your left for the entrance to Catoctin Vineyards. Tours are available on weekends from noon to 5 PM (301-774-2310).

13.7 *Enter the parking lot of the public boat launch and mooring facility.*

Although there are no picnic tables, this is a great spot to rest and view the reservoir. When you've drunk in your fill of the scenery, double back to New Hampshire Avenue.

14.3 *Turn left onto New Hampshire Avenue.*

14.7 *Turn left onto Brighton Dam Road, which is a series of roller-coaster hills.*

15.9 *Turn right into the parking lot of the Brighton Dam office and information center, which has exhibits about the dam and the surrounding area.*

At the end of the parking lot is a soda machine. Steps lead down to a picnic area in the midst of lush, inviting lawns below the dam. There is a playground, and room to fish and walk along the Patuxent River. Across Brighton Dam Road, along the part of the reservoir that spills into the dam, are some azalea gardens developed by dam employees. They are open daily from noon to 7 PM during blooming season.

After a respite, continue on Brighton Dam Road across the dam. Once across, the road begins a steady climb.

17.0 *Turn left onto Nichols Drive.*

18.1 *Turn left onto Highland Road.*

19.0 *Turn left onto Triadelphia Mill Road.*

This is an area of rolling hills and encroaching suburbia, with a few farm holdouts.

20.2 *At the bottom of a hill, Triadelphia Mill Road runs into Greenbridge Road. For a rest by the reservoir, turn left onto Greenbridge Road, which soon turns into easily negotiable, hard-packed gravel.*

20.6 *You'll arrive at the Pig Tail boat-launching area, where the water juts into the land in the shape of a pig's tail.*

This is a nice place to sit under the weeping willows that grow along the bank.

Double back on the same road and continue on the paved portion of Greenbridge Road.

21.1 *Turn left onto Triadelphia Mill Road.*

22.8 *On the left side of the road is a pleasant picnic and boat-launch facility—your last chance to rest by the reservoir on this tour.*

23.5 *Triadelphia Mill Road ends. Turn right onto Triadelphia Road.*

25.2 *Make a sharp left onto Roxbury Road, a rural road lined by cornfields.*

27.5 *Cross Georgia Avenue (MD 97) carefully and turn left onto it, riding on the paved shoulder. Watch for traffic.*

29.6 *Turn right onto Jennings Chapel Road.*

29.9 *Turn left onto Howard Chapel Road.*

This is a scenic and quiet road that runs through undeveloped parkland along the Patuxent River, which is really just a stream at this point. Watch for turtles crossing, and for low-flying goldfinches.

30.4 *The road crosses the Patuxent and reenters Montgomery County.*

The point where the road crosses the stream is a good fishing, wading, and resting spot. The road goes up a slight incline past a horse farm.

32.2 *Cross MD 650.*

32.4 *Turn right onto Sundown Road. Watch for traffic.*

32.9 *Turn left onto Zion Road.*

This is a low-traffic road that leads past Mount Zion Church.

35.9 *Turn right onto Brookeville Road. From now on, you'll be retracing the route you took at the beginning of the trip.*

36.5 *Turn right onto Laytonsville Road (MD 108).*

36.6 *Turn left onto Muncaster Road.*

39.0 *On a hill to your right stands the Magruder Farm.*

Owned by the county, it's used to teach schoolchildren about the area's agricultural past. It started as a tobacco farm in 1734 and later became a wheat farm known as Waveland.

41.7 *Cross Muncaster Mill Road. Muncaster Road continues as Redland Road.*

By this time, you may be ready for some of the fast food available at this intersection.

44.0 *Turn right into the Shady Grove Metro station parking lot.*

Bicycle Repair Service

Griffin Cycle, 3494 Olney-Laytonsville Road, Olney, Maryland (301-774-3970)

COUNTRY ROADS

17
Gunston Gallivant

Location: *Fairfax County, Virginia*
Terrain: *One gradual uphill climb, otherwise flat*
Road conditions: *A short stretch with moderately heavy traffic along Gunston Road, light traffic on paved park roads*
Distance: *9 miles*
Highlights: *Gunston Hall, Mason Neck State Park*

As you make this trip, pretend you are George Mason (1725–1792) making a tour of your 5,000-acre estate. Mason, of course, would have traveled by horse rather than bike, but except for the cars and power-boats, the scene he would have surveyed is much the same: an exquisitely decorated Georgian house, a view of the Potomac River framed by an allée of boxwoods, a peninsula populated by bald eagles, hawks, white-tailed deer, foxes, bobcats, and songbirds.

George Mason was a behind-the-scenes statesman, and once you've experienced the serene beauty of his home, Gunston Hall, and surrounding Mason Neck, you'll understand why he eschewed the political hustle and bustle of Philadelphia and Williamsburg for the quiet of his study. Here, in 1776, he penned the Virginia Declaration of Rights, which helped inspire both our Bill of Rights and France's Declaration of the Rights of Man.

The tour begins at Gunston Hall, which is now owned by the state of Virginia. To get there, take I-95 south from Washington to exit 55, which leads to US 1. Take US 1 south to VA 242. Take VA 242 east to Gunston Hall. Park at the visitors center. Either before or after your bike trip, you'll want to tour the house, outbuildings, and grounds. There is an admission charge, and tours are available daily. Highlights are the Chinese Chippendale dining room and the Palladian parlor, with intri-

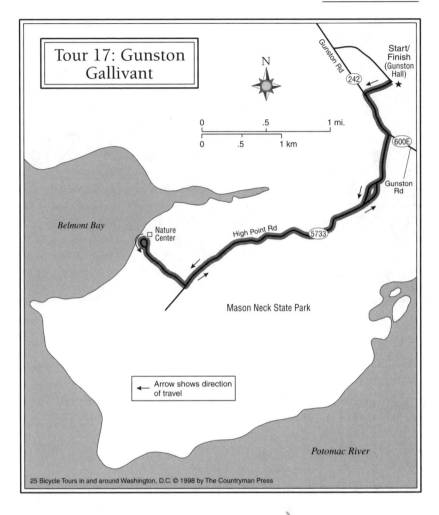

Tour 17: Gunston Gallivant

N

0   .5   1 mi.
0   .5   1 km

Gunston Rd

242

Start/
Finish
(Gunston
Hall)

600E

Gunston
Rd

Belmont Bay

Nature
Center

High Point Rd

5733

Mason Neck State Park

Arrow shows direction
of travel

Potomac River

25 Bicycle Tours in and around Washington, D.C. © 1998 by The Countryman Press

cate carved woodwork by an indentured English servant named William
Buckland.

0.0 *Exit the parking lot and take the entrance road that leads to
Gunston Hall back toward Gunston Road.*

0.6 *Turn left onto Gunston Road (VA 600E). Watch for traffic.*

1.5 *Turn right onto High Point Road (VA 5733) into Mason Neck
Park.*

Visitors are invited to tour the 18th-century mansion and gardens at Gunston Hall, home of colonial statesman George Mason.

This is a lovely road that winds through a heavily wooded area and curves along to the right.

4.5 *The road ends at a nature center on the banks of Belmont Bay.*

The nature center has a slide show and exhibits detailing the natural history of the area, once prime hunting and fishing grounds for the Dogue Indians. In the 19th and 20th centuries, loggers stripped the area of much of the pine and hardwoods, which led to a decline in the bald eagle population. Today, protection of the bald eagles—which have returned in encouraging numbers—is a prime purpose of the park. The fishermen have also returned, both in boats and along the shore. Here you'll find a beach to walk along and miles of hiking trails. You can picnic on the wide lawn that overlooks Belmont Bay, an arm of the Potomac River.

After leaving the nature center area, double back on the park road.

7.5 *Turn left onto Gunston Road (VA 600W). The road makes a gradual climb.*

8.4 Turn right into Gunston Hall.

9.0 Arrive back at the visitors center parking lot.

Bicycle Repair Service

Bikes USA, 14477 Potomac Mills Road, Woodbridge, Virginia (703-494-5300)

18

Two Towns of the Past: Occoquan and Clifton

Location: *Fairfax and Prince William Counties, Virginia*
Terrain: *Hilly*
Road conditions: *Paved roads, some with moderately heavy traffic*
Distance: *29.8 miles*
Highlights: *The historic port of Occoquan, Lorton Reformatory, Fountainhead Regional Park, the landmark town of Clifton*

This tour links two historic towns that have escaped the suburbanization of northern Virginia. Occoquan, once a bustling port and mill town on the banks of the Occoquan River, now bustles instead with shops, restaurants, and art and craft studios. The home of a fleet of pleasure boats, it bursts at the seams each September during a popular craft fair. Its name derives from an Indian word meaning "at the end of the water," and it stands near the point where the Occoquan River runs into the Potomac. The tour follows the river upstream, then goes north to Clifton, another town happily left behind by progress. Clifton is a former railroad center. Its tree-shaded streets hold 68 houses—homes for 200 residents. The entire town is on the National Register of Historic Places, and a sign in front of each building details its history.

Between historic towns, the tour skirts the forbidding Lorton Reformatory, a District of Columbia prison, and travels through both the encroaching suburbia and the surviving farmland of Fairfax County, as well as Fountainhead Regional Park on the Occoquan Reservoir.

The tour begins in Occoquan. To get there, take I-95 south from the Capital Beltway to exit 53. Take VA 123 north for .5 mile to the Occoquan turnoff on your left. Follow signs to the municipal parking lot. You will probably want to bike around the town before setting off on the tour.

The Historic Occoquan Mill House Museum, on Commerce Street, is a good place to learn about Occoquan's past. This building served as the miller's office and is the only remaining part of the once prosperous gristmill that was ravaged by fire in 1916.

European activity in Occoquan began in 1736, when a tobacco warehouse was built. A few decades later, the town was an industrial center with sawmills and the country's first automated gristmill. Grain was taken off ships and barges, processed, then put back on board, ready to be shipped to markets as far away as the West Indies. By 1828 Occoquan also had a cotton mill, one of Virginia's first. Hotels and stores sprang up to serve the farmers, sailors, and traders who flocked here. In the 1850s a shipbuilding industry began in yards along the river. The river was also a source for ice, which was cut and shipped to Washington. The fire of 1916, plus the silting up of the river, began the town's decline. Hurricane Agnes, in 1972, just about completed it. But Occoquan rose again and now has more than 120 shops and restaurants in a compact area.

The mileage count begins at Mill and Union Streets, in front of the Occoquan Inn. If you decide to have a meal there, be sure to check the bathroom on the second floor. The ghost of Occoquan's last Indian is said to make periodic appearances in the mirror.

0.0 Head up Union Street, away from the waterfront.

0.1 Turn left onto Center Street.

0.3 Turn left onto Ox Road (VA 123).

Watch for traffic on this road, which crosses the Occoquan River, climbs a hill, and passes the entrance to Occoquan Regional Park.

1.6 On your right is Lorton Reformatory, a correctional facility run by the District of Columbia. At the V, bear left, continuing on Ox Road.

3.3 Just past the farm stand on your right, turn left onto Hampton Road (VA 647).

This is a quieter road that winds up and down hills, past large homes in wooded settings.

6.3 Turn left into Fountainhead Regional Park.

7.4 You'll find a small snack bar, as well as a dock and boat-rental concession.

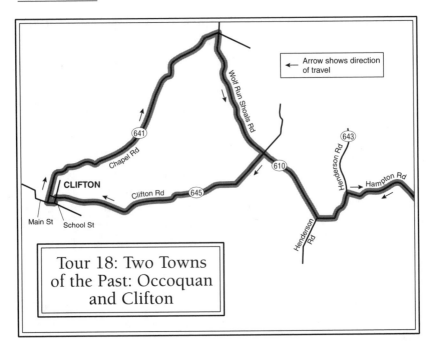

Tour 18: Two Towns of the Past: Occoquan and Clifton

This makes a good rest and picnic stop and affords a view of the lakelike Occoquan Reservoir, formed by Ryans Dam, just upstream on the Occoquan River. This is a favorite spot for fishermen and for people who like to cruise the quiet waters to observe beavers and waterfowl.

8.5 *After doubling back on the park road, turn left onto Hampton Road.*

9.9 *Hampton Road ends. Turn left onto Henderson Road (VA 643).*

10.4 *Turn right onto Wolf Run Shoals Road (VA 610), a straight-away through farm fields.*

11.6 *Turn left onto Clifton Road. Watch for traffic.*
The road winds up and down hills, then passes through a wooded area and descends into Clifton.

14.7 *Turn left onto School Street, then right onto Main Street, which is actually the continuation of Clifton Road.*

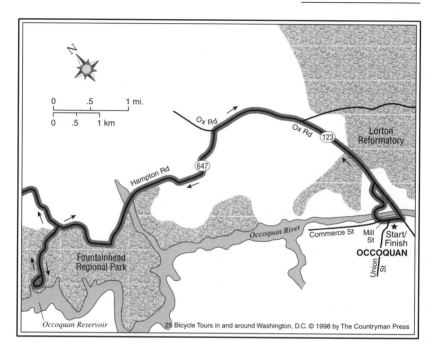

0 .5 1 mi.
0 .5 1 km

Ox Rd

Ox Rd (123)

Lorton Reformatory

Hampton Rd (647)

Occoquan River | Commerce St | Mill St | ★ Start/Finish

OCCOQUAN

Union St

Fountainhead Regional Park

Occoquan Reservoir

25 Bicycle Tours in and around Washington, D.C. © 1998 by The Countryman Press

Main Street has two restaurants, the Hermitage Inn (country French) and the Heart in Hand (southern). For a less formal meal, stop at the Clifton Store, which makes sandwiches to order, and have a picnic in the park behind the Baptist church. The park has a playground, a long sloping lawn, picnic tables, and a gazebo. It is part of the legacy of Clifton's old-fashioned town planning. Most of the houses were built close to the street, with large common areas behind them. Unlike Occoquan, this is a largely residential town, but there are several antiques and craft shops and a children's bookstore to browse through. The town dates from the 1850s, when the Virginia Midland Railroad built a station here. The station was torn down in the 1950s, but the stationmaster's house still stands along the railroad track, a short distance to the left down the dirt road just north of the Clifton Store. This house—like all the others—has a sign in front detailing its history. When the railroad stopped coming here, the town slept for a few decades. But young professionals looking for an alternative to the suburban lifestyle have revived—and preserved—Clifton.

From the Clifton Store, go south on Main Street; then turn left onto Chapel Road.

18.2 *Make a sharp right onto Wolf Run Shoals Road (VA 610).*

21.1 *Turn left onto Henderson Road (VA 643).*

22.4 *Turn right onto Hampton Road (VA 647).*

26.5 *Turn right onto Ox Road (VA 123).*

29.6 *After crossing the Occoquan River, make a sharp right at the Occoquan turnoff.*

29.8 *Return to the parking lot.*

Bicycle Repair Service

Bikes USA, 14477 Potomac Mills Road, Woodbridge, Virginia (703-494-5300)

19
Virginia Vineyards and Views

Location: *Montgomery County in Maryland, and Loudon and Fauquier Counties in Virginia*
Terrain: *Hilly*
Road conditions: *Paved and dirt-and-gravel roads and a paved bike trail*
Distance: *77.6 miles*
Highlights: *The "lost corner" of Virginia, vineyards, the Quaker villages of Waterford and Lincoln, the Washington and Old Dominion Railroad Trail, Middleburg and surrounding horse country, historic Leesburg*

The first day of this trip begins with a ride across the Potomac on an old-fashioned cable ferry and then goes even deeper into the past. After exploring the rural "lost corner" of Virgina and visiting a winery, it winds to the landmark village of Waterford, settled by Pennsylvania Quakers in 1773 and christened by an Irish settler named Thomas Moore a few years later. The tour then makes its way to the Washington and Old Dominion Railroad Trail, then turns south to another Quaker town, Lincoln, for an overnight at a charming and hospitable farm bed & breakfast inn. The next day, the tour makes its way through posh horse country to Middleburg, mecca for the horsey set. After a stop there and an optional loop that takes you to two wineries, the tour follows beautiful Goose Creek along bucolic country roads to Leesburg, which was founded in 1758 and served as the nation's capital for a few days during the War of 1812. From downtown Leesburg, with its wide choice of restaurants and antiques shops, it's a short hop back to the ferry.

An abbreviated version of this trip could be done in a day if you return to Leesburg on the bike trail after Mile 23.3. From this point, it's an easy 6.5 miles to Leesburg and another 4.4 miles to the ferry. You can also shorten the trip by skipping the optional loop to the Piedmont and Meredyth Vineyards from Middleburg.

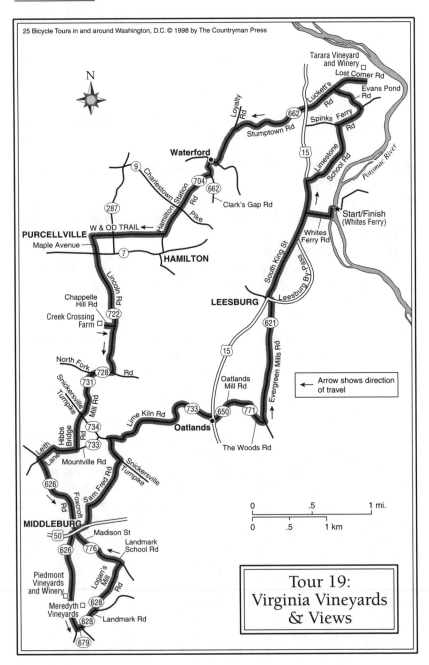

25 Bicycle Tours in and around Washington, D.C. © 1998 by The Countryman Press

N

Tarara Vineyard and Winery

Lost Corner Rd

Evans Pond Rd

Loyalty Rd

Luckett's Rd

Spinks Ferry Rd

662

15

Limestone School Rd

Potomac River

Stumptown Rd

Waterford

9

Charlestown Station Rd

704

662

Clark's Gap Rd

Hamilton Station Pike

287

Start/Finish (Whites Ferry)

W & OD TRAIL

PURCELLVILLE

Maple Avenue

7

HAMILTON

Whites Ferry Rd

South King St

Leesburg By-Pass

LEESBURG

Lincoln Rd

Chappelle Hill Rd

Creek Crossing Farm

722

621

15

North Fork Rd

728

731

Snickersville Turnpike

Mill Rd

Oatlands Mill Rd

Evergreen Mills Rd

Arrow shows direction of travel

Lime Kiln Rd

733

650

771

Oatlands

734

Hibbs Bridge Rd

733

The Woods Rd

Leith Lane

Mountville Rd

Snickersville Turnpike

626

Sam Fred Rd

Foxcroft Rd

0   .5   1 mi.

0   .5   1 km

MIDDLEBURG

50

Madison St

Landmark School Rd

626

776

Logan's Mill Rd

Piedmont Vineyards and Winery

Meredyth Vineyards

628

628

Landmark Rd

679

Tour 19: Virginia Vineyards & Views

To get to Whites Ferry from the Beltway, take I-270 to the MD 28 exit and follow MD 28 in the direction of Darnestown. Continue to Dawsonville and turn left onto Whites Ferry Road (MD 107). The ferry is at the end of the road and runs year-round, seven days a week, from 5 AM until well past dark. During unusually high water, the ferry may not be able to cross. For information, call 301-349-5200. The ferry has a large parking lot and a store.

Day I

0.0 Ride off the ferry on the Virginia shore, following Whites Ferry Road, which is lined with wild bluebells in spring.

1.2 Turn right onto US 15N, riding on the shoulder.

2.6 Turn right onto Limestone School Road, which is hard-packed dirt and gravel with little traffic. It winds through woods and past farms.

On your left is the entrance to Temple Hall Farm Regional Park, an outdoor education facility for school groups that is open to the general public only on special occasions. (Call 703-729-0596 for information.) The pleasant manor house was built around 1810 by a nephew of George Mason, author of Virginia's Declaration of Rights (see Tour 17). It was restored by the Symington family in the 1940s and donated to the park authority in 1985. It showcases Virginia's farming heritage and houses many farm animals, including goats, pigs, and sheep.

Continue on Limestone School Road, which affords views of Maryland's Sugarloaf Mountain to your right and passes large horse farms.

6.3 Turn right onto Spinks Ferry Road, which is also dirt and gravel. You are now in Virginia's "lost corner," a rural area of farms and country homes high above the Potomac River.

7.6 Turn left onto Evans Pond Road, which is paved.

9.1 Turn right onto Lucketts Road (VA 662).

This road is a ribbon through a broad agricultural valley rimmed by blue mountains.

127

9.7 *Lucketts Road becomes Lost Corner Road and bears right, through a small settlement and past vineyards.*

10.6 *Turn left into Tarara (Ararat spelled backward) Vineyard and Winery.*

The winery offers tours Thursday through Monday from 11 to 5. The 60-acre site overlooks the Potomac and produces Chardonnays, Cabernets, and other fine wines.

After your tour, reverse direction on Lost Corner Road.

11.5 *Lost Corner Road becomes Lucketts Road.*

13.6 *Lucketts Road crosses US 15.*

At the intersection are several antiques shops and a gas station. Past the intersection, Lucketts Road becomes Stumptown Road, which winds mainly uphill but affords some exhilarating downhill runs.

17.2 *Turn left onto Loyalty Road, which leads into Waterford. Bear left onto Water Street (VA 698), then turn right onto Main Street.*

Pennsylvania Quakers settled Waterford in 1773, but the town got its name a few years later when Irish settler Thomas Moore persuaded his neighbors to call the growing village after his hometown back in Ireland. Waterford served the surrounding farms, providing such services as milling, tanning, and coachmaking. The entire village is now a National Historic Landmark. Many of the historic homes are open for tours on one weekend in October. Contact the Waterford Foundation (703-882-3018) for information and for a map to use for walking tours, or pick one up at any of the shops. Of particular interest are the mill, the weaver's cottage, the tin shop, the Second Street School, and the jail.

19.2 *At the post office, make a sharp left onto 2nd Street, which curves past more beautiful homes and becomes Factory Street.*

19.3 *Turn right onto Clark's Gap Road (VA 662), which is busy.*

19.9 *Turn right onto Hamilton Station Road (VA 704).*

The road winds mainly uphill past farms and posh new homes. The road crosses Charles Town Pike (VA 9) and ends at the defunct Hamilton station on the Washington and Old Dominion. Trains once brought Washingtonians to this station for summer respites in the Quaker hamlet of Hamilton.

23.3 *Turn right onto the W&OD Trail, which is wooded on both sides.*

Watch for cattle, which sometimes wander close to get a better view of the action.

25.4 *The trail emerges from the woods and seems to end, but it doesn't. Follow the marked path along VA 287, crossing at the crosswalk and continuing on the trail toward Purcellville.*

26.6 *Exit the trail at Maple Avenue, bearing left, past a firehouse and some fast-food establishments. Cross VA 7 (Business) at the light, after which Maple Avenue becomes Lincoln Road (VA 722).*

Follow Lincoln Road through a pleasant residential area and into the country.

28.0 *After passing through the small Quaker settlement of Lincoln, turn right onto Chappelle Hill Road.*

28.1 *Take the first farm entrance into Creek Crossing Farm.*

The farm offers bed & breakfast on a 20-acre farm (see *Accommodations*). The restored 18th-century farmhouse sits on a hill and is furnished with antiques. After a refreshing night at the inn, the tour continues on to Middleburg.

Day 2

28.2 *After leaving the B&B, turn left onto Chappelle Hill Road and right onto Lincoln Road.*

31.6 *Turn right onto North Fork Road (VA 728).*

32.3 *Turn left onto Mill Road (VA 731), looking to your right for sweeping mountain views.*

34.4 *Turn left onto Snickersville Turnpike (VA 734), which leads downhill and across a bridge.*

34.5 *Turn right onto Hibbs Bridge Road, which is hard-packed dirt* *and gravel but very scenic, running through woods above a stream.*

35.9 *Turn right onto Mountville Road (VA 733), which is paved.*

37.0 *Bear left onto Leith Lane.*

37.8 *Turn left onto Foxcroft Road (VA 626), which winds its way up and down hills past the posh horse farms that Middleburg is famous for.*

40.3 *On your left is Glenwood Park, a public park that hosts point-to-point steeplechase races accompanied by elegant tailgate picnics in spring and fall.*

41.6 *Foxcroft Road ends. Bear right at Mosby's Tavern.*

This popular restaurant and watering hole was named for Col. John Mosby, the Confederate irregular who operated hereabouts. At the tavern, turn left onto Madison Street. On your right is The Pink Box, an information center staffed by helpful volunteers. Rest rooms are available, and there's a beautiful garden dedicated to Jacqueline Kennedy, who used to ride in the Middleburg area.

Middleburg dates from 1731, when a cousin of George Washington opened a tavern on Ashby's Gap Turnpike. The turnpike is now known as US 50 and the tavern as the Red Fox. Today Middleburg is the site of multimillion-dollar horse farms and a few wineries. Horse farms welcome the public only once a year, usually Memorial Day weekend, in a stable tour that benefits Trinity Episcopal Church in nearby Upperville.

For a dining alternative to Mosby's Tavern and the Red Fox Inn, turn right at the intersection of US 50 and go one block to the Upper Crust Bakery, which offers delicious sandwiches and freshly baked pies and cookies. Outdoor tables are available.

After your meal, reverse direction on US 50. To skip the optional loop to the wineries, continue east on this road and pick up the rest of the tour at Mile 52.8.

42.5 *If you wish to visit two local wineries, turn right onto VA 626. You'll climb and descend some hills and pass large estates with horse pastures protected by stone fences.*

45.3 *Turn right into Piedmont Vineyards and Winery.*

Creek Crossing Farm, a working farm with a restored 1773 house, offers bed and breakfast to cyclists and others.

Pass the sign requesting DO NOT BOTHER SWANS and the mellow, yellow Waverly, a landmark pre–Revolutionary War mansion and residence of the Furness family, which founded the vineyard in 1973. Although Virginians, including Thomas Jefferson, had long sought to establish wineries, this was the first commercial vinifera vineyard in the state. The 36-acre vineyard is planted with Chardonnay, Semillon, and Seyval Blanc grapes.

45.5 Park at the old dairy barn that now houses the winery and sales room.

It's open Tuesday through Sunday 10 AM to 4 PM. Tours and tastings are informal and free. A guide will walk you through the wine-making process and show you the machines that press the grapes, the stainless-steel tanks where the juice, or "must," is placed in order to allow the suspended solid matter to settle out, and the temperature-controlled oak fermenting barrels. Piedmont produces about 7,000 cases of wine a year. The output includes two Chardonnays, a Semillon, and two white wines made from the Seyval Blanc grape. Little River White is semidry, and Hunt Country White is dry. You'll be invited to taste several wines, and you'll probably want to buy a bottle for your picnic. Since biking and drinking aren't compatible, go easy on the tasting.

Just outside the winery are picnic tables. As you picnic with Waverly as a backdrop, don't be surprised to have horses looking over your shoulder.

After the tour, continue south on VA 626.

45.9 *Turn left onto VA 679 (not well marked; easy to miss).*

46.0 *VA 679 ends. Bear left onto VA 628 (Landmark Road).*

47.1 *VA 628 meets VA 686 at a V. Bear left, remaining on VA 628 (Logans Mill Road).*

47.4 *Take a left at the Meredyth Vineyards sign and follow the dirt road.*

The road leads through the 56-acre vineyard, set against the spectacular backdrop of the Bull Run Mountains. On your way in, you'll come to some picturesque picnic grounds, complete with ruins of old stone buildings, but you may want to wait until you've taken the tour and purchased some wine.

47.8 *Park in front of the winery, a large green barn.*

Tours are available daily 10 AM–4 PM (except Christmas, Easter, Thanksgiving, and New Year's Day). Meredyth produces an impressive variety of wines, including Seyval Blanc, Villard Blanc, Riesling, Chardonnay, Cabernet Sauvignon, and Merlot, from its French-American hybrids, and the winery puts on a good tour..

48.2 *Exit the vineyard and go left onto VA 628.*

The road is loosely packed gravel with lots of hills.

50.2 *Turn left onto VA 776 (Landmark School Road). This runs into*

Madison Street in Middleburg.

52.8 *Turn right onto US 50.*

53.5 *At St. Stephen's Catholic Church, turn left onto Sam Fred Road (VA 748), which rolls through wooded hills.*

56.9 *Sam Fred Road ends at Cotswald Farm, a major horse farm. Turn left onto Snickersville Turnpike (VA 734).*

58.0 *At the T, turn right onto Lime Kiln Road (VA 733).*

The road turns to dirt and gravel and winds through picturesque woods and farmland beside Goose Creek.

61.5 *Pavement resumes and the road gets wider.*

63.6 *Lime Kiln Road ends in the small crossroads of Oatlands, at US 15.*

Note: The mansion of the same name is not right here and you would have an unpleasant ride on busy US 15 to reach it.

Cross US 15 and ride on the shoulder past the Episcopal Church of Our Savior.

63.7 *Turn left onto Oatlands Mill Road (VA 650), also a picturesque rural dirt road.*

65.1 *At the crossroads, continue straight on The Woods Road (VA 771).*

The road winds uphill through deep woods and there are some rough patches of gravel.

66.9 *The Woods Road ends on Evergreen Mills Road (VA 621). Turn left onto this paved road leading through increasingly suburban areas into Leesburg.*

72.1 *Evergreen Mills Road ends at South King Street. Turn right onto South King Street, taking care to avoid the cars that are turning in to the Leesburg By-Pass.*

73.2 *King Street crosses the W&OD bike trail and leads into downtown Leesburg.*

Founded in 1758 and named for Lightfoot Harry Lee, the town served as the nation's capital for a few days during the War of 1812: The Constitution and the Declaration of Independence were brought here for safekeeping. The picturesque, mellow, redbrick town offers a variety of antiques shops and eating places.

After a respite, continue up King Street (US 15 Business). Be careful when it rejoins US 15 and ride on the shoulder.

76.4 Turn right onto Whites Ferry Road.

77.6 Ride onto the ferry and cross the Potomac, returning to the parking lot.

Bicycle Repair Service

Bicycle Outfitters, 19 Catoctin Circle NE, Leesburg, Virginia (703-777-6126)

Accommodations

Creek Crossing Farm at Chappelle Hill, Lincoln, Virginia (540-338-7550)

20

By the Old Mill Stream

Location: The Shenandoah Valley of Virginia (Clarke County)
Terrain: Roller-coaster hills with some flat stretches
Road conditions: Light traffic on paved roads
Distance: 27.7 miles
Highlights: The restored Burwell-Morgan Mill, antiques shops, the
Shenandoah River

This tour is especially fun in the summer, since, after you've mastered
the roller-coaster hills, you can cool off in the clean, fresh Shenandoah.
(Because there's no place to change, you might want to wear a swimsuit
under your clothes.) In the shadow of the Blue Ridge, this is apple, horse,
and cattle country, with hilly farms marked off by stone fences. Except
during hunting season, you're likely to spot some deer.

The tour begins in Millwood, an 18th-century town with lovely old
homes, a restored and working mill, and several antiques shops. To reach
Millwood, take I-66 west to US 17 north. Follow US 17 to the intersection with US 50. Take US 50 west. Just after you cross the Shenandoah
River, turn right onto VA 723. The Burwell-Morgan Mill is on your left
in Millwood. Leave your car in the parking lot.

**0.0 After visiting the mill, exit the parking lot and turn right onto
VA 723.**

The Burwell-Morgan Mill, completed in 1785 by two men who
met serving in the Revolutionary War, once catered to the local
wheat-growing community. Today it grinds and sells cornmeal and
serves picnickers and history buffs. During the Civil War, troops
from both armies bought flour—and swapped yarns—here. It
ceased operations in 1953 and was later restored by the Clarke

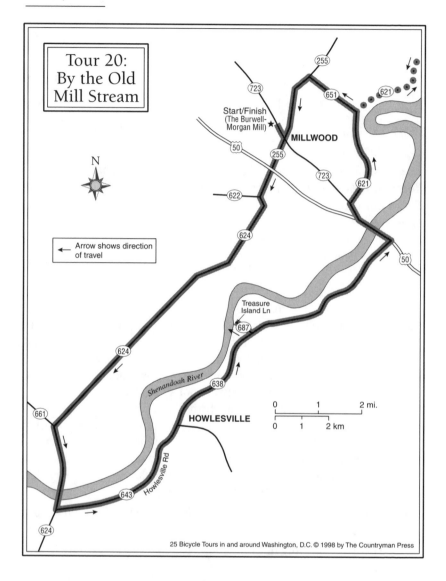

Tour 20:
By the Old
Mill Stream

N

Arrow shows direction
of travel

Start/Finish
(The Burwell-
Morgan Mill)

MILLWOOD

Treasure
Island Ln

Shenandoah River

HOWLESVILLE

Howlesville Rd

0   1   2 mi.
0   1   2 km

25 Bicycle Tours in and around Washington, D.C. © 1998 by The Countryman Press

County Historical Association. A small donation is requested for a tour of the 40-by-60-foot building, with its indoor overshot water-wheel, wooden gears, and French grindstones. Barrels of flour were once stored in the building until the waters of the Shen-andoah were high enough to float them in flatboats to Harpers

Ferry. (See Tour 26.) From there they were put on canal boats bound for Georgetown. (You can buy the mill's cornmeal in small bags, each imprinted with a picture of the building.) The mill uses the waters of Spout Run, which is lined with willows that shelter several picnic tables on the lush green. Adjacent to the mill is Brookside Bed and Breakfast and Antiques, built in 1780. Several more antiques shops are within walking distance.

0.2 Turn right onto VA 255.

0.8 Cross US 50 carefully. On the other side of US 50, the road becomes VA 624. Follow it through the intersection with VA 622.

This stretch of road consists of roller-coaster hills through farm country, with mountains on your right and hills sloping down toward the river on your left.

7.7 VA 624 turns left for an enjoyable and well-earned downhill run to the river.

9.0 Cross the wide Shenandoah on a low, narrow bridge. Continue on VA 624, climbing uphill slightly.

You will probably see cows wading in the river. On the other side of the river there's a boat launch, and this is a very popular fishing spot. You could wade or swim here, but there's a better spot farther along.

9.3 Turn left onto VA 643, Howlesville Road. After passing through the small settlement of Howlesville, VA 643 becomes VA 638.

This road is less picturesque, but also less hilly, than the road on the other side of the river.

15.2 Turn left onto VA 687, Treasure Island Lane, a suburban-like street that ends in a cul-de-sac at Mile 15.4.

Lock your bike to a tree or push it along the dirt path down to a tributary of the river. A defunct and deteriorating pedestrian bridge hangs over the water in a cool, green, Corot-like glade. You can picnic or wade here, but for deeper, wider water, follow the stream to your right, walking in the water for about a quarter of a mile to the intersection with the Shenandoah. This is a great spot for a swim, and since there's no road access, it definitely won't be crowded. After lingering here as long as time allows, return to your bike and double back up Treasure Island Lane.

Whether you're traveling on four legs or two wheels, a dip in the
Shenandoah offers a refreshing respite.

15.6 *Turn left onto VA 638.*

16.6 *You'll find a grocery store on your right.*

19.8 *Cross US 50 and turn left onto it. Ride on the shoulder across
the Shenandoah.*

20.3 *Take a right onto VA 723 and then an immediate right onto
VA 621.*

This is a scenic country road that winds through farm country, up
and down small hills. Watch for deer in the fields.

23.6 *At the intersection with VA 651, VA 621 continues as a dirt
road along the river.*

If you want to take another swim, follow this road for a few hundred yards. To continue the tour, turn left at the intersection onto
VA 651, which climbs a medium-sized hill.

25.4 *Turn left onto VA 255.*

25.6 *On your left, private but visible from the road, stands Carter Hall.*

This stone manor house was built by Lt. Col. Nathaniel Burwell,
one of the owners of the Burwell-Morgan Mill. The house was

built in 1792 and named for Burwell's former home, Carter's Grove, one of the famous James River plantations. In 1862 Stonewall Jackson set up headquarters here, but refused an invitation to stay in the house. Instead, he camped on the lawn with his troops. Across the road is Christ Episcopal Church, which dates from 1832. Lovely old homes—some modest, some grand—line the road as it approaches Millwood.

27.6 *Just before the intersection with VA 723, you will see an old red schoolhouse, built in 1858, that now houses an antiques store.*

27.6 *Turn right onto VA 723.*

27.7 *Turn left into the mill parking lot.*

Bicycle Repair Service

Winchester Bicycle Center, 2040 South Pleasant Valley Road, Winchester, Virginia (540-662-5744)

21
Cruising around Croom

Location: *Prince George's County, Maryland*
Terrain: *Almost flat*
Road conditions: *Park roads and country roads with light traffic*
Distance: *28.5 miles*
Highlights: *Patuxent River Park, Merkle Wildlife Sanctuary, St. Thomas Church*

This tour takes you to a part of Maryland's Prince George's County that's still country—a place where tobacco still grows, osprey still nest, and where the Canada geese come to eat the wild rice and end up staying the winter. The tour begins at Patuxent River Park, where the Patuxent River widens into Jug Bay. Following the Chesapeake Bay Critical Areas Drive, the tour visits the first airfield in the United States owned and operated by an African American and stops at an observation tower over a tidal marsh. After a stop at St. Thomas Church, completed in 1745, the tour takes in Merkle Wildlife Sanctuary and Visitor Center, which hosts hummingbirds and Canada geese, and continues to now nonexistent Nottingham, a hotbed of intrigue and activity during the War of 1812. After a look at Mattaponi, built in 1745 by the Bowie family, the trip ends back in Patuxent River Park.

To get to Patuxent River Park from the Beltway, take MD 4 to US 301 south. Take US 301 to Croom Road (MD 382), then take Croom Road south to Croom Airport Road. Turn left onto Croom Airport Road and continue to the park entrance. Leave your car in the lot near the park office.

Either before or after your bike ride, you'll want to enjoy some of the attractions of this 2,000-acre park—by taking a stroll on the boardwalk that leads through the wetlands and by touring the Patuxent village, an exhibit that depicts life on the river in the 19th century. Check at the

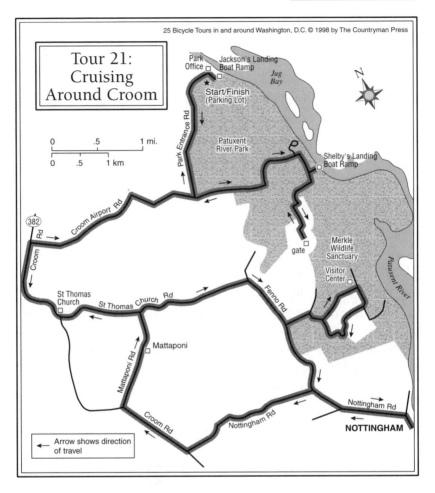

Tour 21: Cruising Around Croom

25 Bicycle Tours in and around Washington, D.C. © 1998 by The Countryman Press

park office for a schedule of events. By calling ahead (301-627-6094), you may be able to make arrangements for canoeing or camping or for a ride on an electric boat.

0.0 Exit the parking lot and head back out the park entrance road.

1.7 Turn left onto Croom Airport Road, which winds to the left down a hill.

2.4 At the bottom of the hill, turn left, following the signs for Selby's Landing Boat Ramp.

3.1 **A sign in a field marks the site of the Columbia Air Center.**

The first airfield owned and operated by a black, it was opened in 1941 by John W. Greene Jr. During World War II, the Navy used the field for training.

3.7 **Selby's Landing Boat Ramp has a dock if you want to sit by the river.**

4.8 **The road turns to a wooden bridge over a freshwater tidal marsh.**

An observation tower allows you to watch for the birds, muskrats, and diamondback terrapin that frequent the marsh. Serious birders sometimes set up telescopes on the bridge. They appreciate quiet. On the other side of the bridge is Merkle Wildlife Sanctuary. Dirt roads lead to the visitors center, but bicycles are not allowed on them except during specified times. Currently, cyclists and hikers may use this route on summer Saturdays from 10 to 3. Call 301-888-1410 for up-to-date information.

Otherwise, you need to backtrack to the entrance of Patuxent River Park on Croom Airport Road.

7.9 **At the park entrance, continue on Croom Airport Road.**

9.9 **Turn left onto Croom Road.**

10.8 **Turn left onto St. Thomas Church Road.**

On your left, immediately after the turn, is the church, completed in 1745 but with Victorian alterations. In the churchyard, among the pines and cedars, are graves of some of the first families of Maryland: Bowies and Calverts and Duvalls. There is also a memorial to a former rector, Thomas John Claggett, who later became the first Episcopalian bishop consecrated in the United States. Inscribed on the memorial is a quote from Claggett: "How awesome is the dawn sky over the hills of Croom . . . It makes my heart sing 'praised be God.' "

13.2 **Turn right onto Fenno Road.**

This is a rural road that parallels the river.

13.9 **Turn left into Merkle Wildlife Sanctuary and follow the one-way loop to the visitors center.**

Merkle was a local farmer and wildlife lover who donated this property for conservation purposes. The center is open 10 to 4, Tuesday through Sunday and has exhibits on the river and the animals found in its watershed. A special feature is a hummingbird garden with telescopes set up so you can view the tiny birds at close range. There is also a pond favored by visiting waterfowl.

After your visit, return to Fenno Road, completing the one-way loop.

15.7 *Turn left onto Fenno Road.*

17.6 *Turn left onto Nottingham Road.*

This road ends at the river, but with no access. Nottingham, which now consists of only a few houses, was once a thriving port. During the War of 1812, it served as headquarters for Commodore Joshua Barney, whose flotilla was bottled up here by the British fleet. Secretary of State James Monroe reportedly donned cloak and dagger and came to Nottingham to size up the British forces, who were advancing up the Patuxent and camped in Nottingham the night of August 21, 1814.

Turn around and backtrack on Nottingham Road, continuing past the intersection with Fenno Road, through tobacco-farming country.

20.7 *Turn right onto Croom Road (MD 382).*

21.6 *Turn right onto Mattaponi Road.*

22.3 *Mattoponi, built around 1745, is on your right.*

The 2½-story hip-roofed house was once the ancestral home of the Bowies, some of whom are buried in St. Thomas churchyard. Today, it's owned by the Catholic Church.

22.8 *Turn left onto St. Thomas Church Road and follow it up a small hill, past the church.*

23.7 *Turn right onto Croom Road.*

24.8 *Turn right onto Croom Airport Road.*

26.8 *Turn left into Patuxent River Park.*

28.5 *Return to the parking lot.*

Bicycle Repair Service

Family Bicycles, 416 Hampton Park Boulevard, Capitol Heights, Maryland (301-350-0903)

22
Getaway to Galesville

Location: *Prince George's and Anne Arundel Counties in Maryland*
Metro access: *New Carrollton*
Terrain: *Rolling to moderately hilly*
Road conditions: *Paved roads, most with little traffic*
Distance: *51.4 miles*
Highlights: *Historic churches; the Old Quaker Burying Ground; Galesville, with its restaurants, antiques shops, and waterfront parks*

Galesville, long a popular boating destination for Washingtonians, also makes a good bike-trip destination. It's probably the nearest Chesapeake Bay town to Washington—although it's actually on the West River near the point where the river joins the bay.

Galesville, established in 1684, was an active port during the steamboat era. Today it is a stately old town with large frame houses lining the main street. Its economy is based on an oyster cannery, plus a lot of businesses that serve visiting boaters, including marinas and restaurants. What makes the town a nice place to visit is that some of its waterfront has been set aside as parkland, making it available for picnicking.

The tour starts at the New Carrollton Metro station, terminus of the Orange Line, and quickly takes the rider into the country.

0.0 *Exit the New Carrollton station on the east side, following the bus lane. At the exit, turn right onto Garden City Drive, then left at the V, under US 50. Continue to the left onto Ardwick Ardmore Road.*

At first the road is lined with factories and other light industries, but it soon turns more countrylike.

3.3 *Ardwick Ardmore Road ends in front of the Enterprise Golf Course. Turn right onto Lottsford Vista Road.*

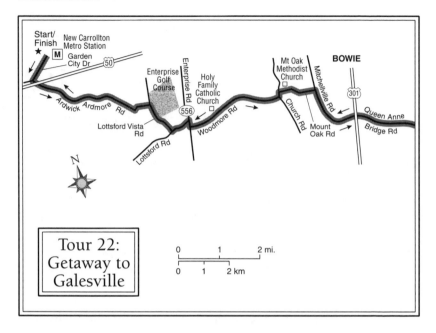

Tour 22:
Getaway to
Galesville

0   1   2 mi.

0   1   2 km

4.5 *Lottsford Vista Road ends. Turn left onto Lottsford Road.*

5.2 *Lottsford Road ends at Enterprise Road (MD 556). Cross Enterprise Road—carefully—and continue straight ahead on Woodmore Road.*

5.7 *The white-clapboard Holy Family Catholic Church, set amid tall trees, dates from 1890.*

8.1 *Woodmore Road ends at Church Road. On your right is the Mount Oak Methodist Church Cemetery, established in 1890. Turn left onto Church Road; then make an immediate right onto Mount Oak Road.*

On your left, just after the turn, is the Mount Oak Methodist Church, built in 1881. The road continues over rolling hills in a country setting.

9.8 *Turn right onto Mitchellville Road after stopping at the shopping center at the intersection for food if desired.*

You have reentered suburbia, the greater Bowie area.

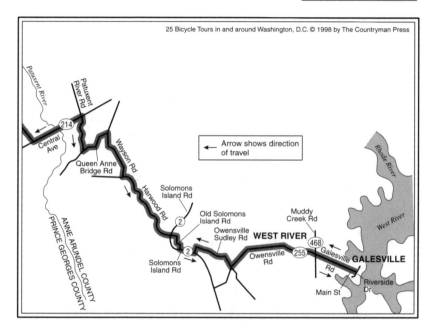

25 Bicycle Tours in and around Washington, D.C. © 1998 by The Countryman Press

11.1 *Proceed carefully across US 301 and its large center island. At the other side of the highway, Mitchellville Road becomes Queen Anne Bridge Road.*

After a brief uphill climb, the road rolls through a pleasant rural area.

13.2 *Turn left onto Central Avenue (MD 214). Watch for traffic.*

After crossing the Patuxent River, you'll enter Anne Arundel County.

14.5 *Turn right onto Patuxent River Road.*

15.4 *Turn left onto Queen Anne Bridge Road.*

16.6 *Make a sharp right onto Wayson Road in front of the National Guard installation.*

This stretch features roller-coaster hills.

17.9 *Turn left onto Harwood Road, which runs through cornfields and crosses shady Stocketts Run.*

20.3 *Cross Solomons Island Road (MD 2) at Harwood Post Office.*

Enter Old Solomons Island Road.

This is a rural loop that will minimize the time you have to spend on busy MD 2.

20.8 **Old Solomons Island Road ends. Turn left onto Solomons Island Road (MD 2). Ride on the shoulder.**

21.0 **Turn left onto Owensville Sudley Road, which soon makes a right turn and travels through farm country.**

22.3 **Turn left onto Owensville Road (MD 255).**

Christ Church Parish Hall, at the intersection, has a big front yard with a towering oak to rest under. Next door is the Episcopal church itself, a white frame structure with a boxwood-scented cemetery.

Leaving the town of West River, Owensville Road winds mainly downhill past tobacco farms and their weathered gray barns. The vertical slats on the barns slant open to allow air-drying of the hanging tobacco leaves.

24.7 **Owensville Road crosses Muddy Creek Road (MD 468) and becomes Galesville Road.**

On your right, just before the intersection, is a gas station and convenience store. Across the intersection lies the Old Quaker Burying Ground, founded in 1672, which may be explored through a gate in the picket fence, if you have the time and the inclination. A Quaker meetinghouse that once stood here burned during the Civil War.

25.5 **R&M Antiques (left) is chock-full of china, bric-a-brac, and other old things. The store is the former home of the Pink Domain Antique Store.**

25.6 **You arrive at the West River Market & Deli on your left.**

The market has groceries and excellent carryout sandwiches, and the building also houses a gift and antiques shop. There are picnic tables in the yard, but you may want to bring your sandwiches down to the waterfront. Next door to the market are two art galleries, and across the road is a marker showing that William Penn passed this way to board a boat across the Chesapeake.

25.7 **The road meets the waterfront, where there is a small park.**

Although it's nearly impossible to cart antiques away by bicycle, the Pink Domain, now called R&M Antiques, in Galesville, Maryland, is well worth a browse.

You may picnic here, or try one of Galesville's several restaurants, all of which feature seafood. The Topside Inn is on the left at the intersection of MD 255 and Riverside Drive. A few hundred yards to the right is Steamboat Landing, a restaurant set on pilings in the river. It offers informal outdoor dining and will also arrange boat rides. Turn left onto Riverside Drive to Pirates Cove (right), which offers both food and lodging. Just past Pirates Cove, sandwiched between a marina and the West River Sailing Club, stands narrow Elizabeth Dixon Park, which features two picnic tables under a tree by the water. When you finish admiring the view of the West and Rhode Rivers flowing into Chesapeake Bay, read the poem by Elizabeth Dixon that's engraved on a plaque set in a rock. A sampling reads: "Even the sun has a broken path/ As it glistens across the sea./ But the bright spot in the path it seems/ Is always the furthest from me."

Ideally, you should linger awhile in Galesville, boat-watching from the deck of the Steamboat Landing Restaurant as you sip a Bloody Mary with Old Bay seasoning dusted around the rim of the glass. You could dine here on crabs or other local fare, and spend the night—either in the Inn at Pirates Cove (301-261-5050) or at Oakwood, an 1840 manor house that now offers bed & breakfast (301-261-5338). If you must get back to Washington, however, you'll have to cut short your visit to get home before dark. Although alternative routes were explored, none are recommended, so you'll have to reverse direction.

29.1 *Turn right onto Owensville Sudley Road.*

30.4 *Turn right onto MD 2 (Solomons Island Road).*

30.6 *Turn right onto Old Solomons Island Road.*

31.1 *Old Solomons Island Road ends. Cross MD 2 and enter Harwood Road.*

33.5 *Turn right onto Wayson Road.*

34.8 *Turn left onto Queen Anne Bridge Road.*

36.0 *Turn right onto Patuxent River Road.*

36.9 *Turn left onto MD 214. Watch for traffic.*

38.2 *Turn right onto Queen Anne Bridge Road.*

40.3 *After you cross US 301, Queen Anne Bridge Road becomes Mitchellville Road. Continue on Mitchellville Road.*

41.6 *Turn left onto Mount Oak Road.*

43.2 *Turn left onto Church Road, then make an immediate right onto Woodmore Road.*

46.2 *Cross Enterprise Road. Woodmore Road becomes Lottsford Road.*

46.9 *Turn right onto Lottsford Vista Road.*

48.1 *Turn left onto Ardwick Ardmore Road.*

51.1 *Following the "M" for Metro signs, turn left onto Pennsy Drive and cross the bridge.*

51.3 *Turn left onto Corporate Drive.*

51.4 *Arrive at New Carrollton Metro station.*

Bicycle Repair Service

Family Bicycles, 416 Hampton Park Boulevard, Capitol Heights, Maryland (301-350-0903)

A&M Cycle, 13002 9th Street, Bowie, Maryland (301-262-4343)

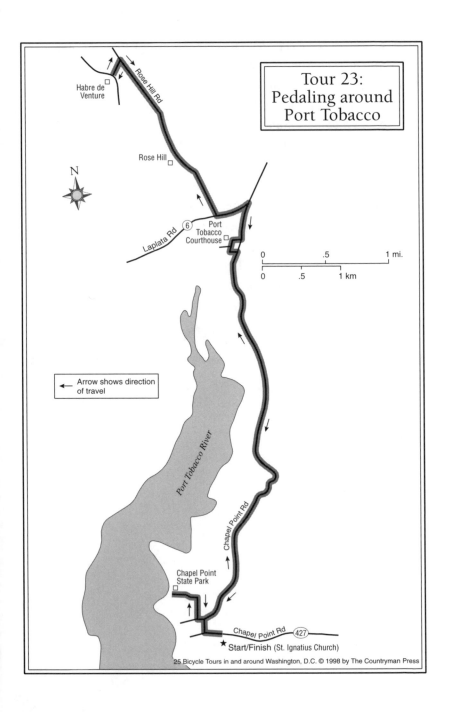

Tour 23:
Pedaling around
Port Tobacco

Habre de
Venture

Rose Hill Rd

Rose Hill

N

Laplata Rd

6 Port
Tobacco
Courthouse

0   .5   1 mi.

0   .5   1 km

Arrow shows direction
of travel

Port Tobacco River

Chapel Point Rd

Chapel Point
State Park

Chapel Point Rd   427

★ Start/Finish (St. Ignatius Church)

25 Bicycle Tours in and around Washington, D.C. © 1998 by The Countryman Press

23
Pedaling around Port Tobacco

Location: Charles County, Maryland
Terrain: Rolling hills, with some flat stretches
Road conditions: Paved country roads with light traffic
Distance: 12.4 miles
Highlights: St. Ignatius Roman Catholic Church and cemetery, Chapel Point State Park, Port Tobacco courthouse and museum, the Thomas Stone National Historic Site

The ghost town of Port Tobacco provides a glimpse into Maryland's 18th-century past—when tobacco was king, rivers were roads, and life revolved around gracious plantation homes, many of which are still standing. Founded on the site of an Indian village with a name that sounded like Potobac to the first European settlers, the town soon lived up to its name, shipping out hogsheads of tobacco on ships that sailed in and out of the port. The economy, based on slave labor, supported lavish plantations. When the Civil War took away both soldiers and slaves, the area began to decline. Nature also contributed to the town's demise when the river silted up, stranding the old port. A debate over moving the courthouse west to La Plata, which was served by the railroad, was settled in 1891 when the Port Tobacco courthouse "mysteriously" burned down. The arsonists had thoughtfully moved the records outside, and they were later transferred to La Plata, now the county seat.

Although deserted, the town is not gloomy. You can tour the restored courthouse and museum and one of the few remaining houses. You can also inspect St. Ignatius church and its cemetery, wander the beach along the river, look at the historic manor houses of Rose Hill, from the road, and Habre de Venture, from closer up.

Start your tour at St. Ignatius Roman Catholic Church, Chapel Point, which has a parking lot. To reach the starting point from the Beltway, take MD 5 south to US 301. Take US 301 south through La Plata to the intersection with MD 427 (Chapel Point Road). Turn right onto Chapel Point Road to the church.

0.0 *From St. Ignatius, continue west on Chapel Point Road, down a short, steep hill, and around a sharp curve.*

Rosy redbrick St. Ignatius church was built in 1789 on the site of a chapel built by Father Andrew White, who sailed into Maryland with the first group of settlers in 1634. The adjacent manor house, which dates from 1741, was built on the site of an earlier home. It has been occupied since then by Jesuits, many of whom are buried in the nearby graveyard. The graveyard, which slopes down toward the river, is a peaceful place that affords an unsurpassed view of the river, the lush countryside, and, on a hill up the river, Rose Hill, once the home of one of George Washington's doctors.

0.5 *Take a left at the sign into Chapel Point State Park. The road will curve right, then left to the river, a parking lot, and a pebbly beach.*

The sign says NO SWIMMING but fishing is allowed and you can wander along the beach and at least wade. Past the duck blind to your left there's a shady picnic site.

Retrace your steps to the entrance to the park.

0.9 *Turn left at the park exit onto Chapel Point Road.*

This slightly rolling road leads past tobacco farms, woods, and a few suburban-type dwellings.

4.8 *At the historical marker, turn left into the old courthouse square.*

Most of the homes around the square, with 18th-century dates on them, are privately owned and inhabited. After securing your bike, however, you can visit the restored courthouse and museum for a nominal fee. It's open June through August, Wednesday through Sunday noon to 4 PM, and April, May, and September through December, weekends noon to 4 PM. The museum contains a mock-up of the large settlement, including hotels and tobacco warehouses that once thrived here, as well as gleanings from an archaeological dig. You'll find one whimsical exhibit: broken-off clay pipe stems. It seems that hotel guests, after smoking, would break off the mouthpiece, leaving a germ-free pipe for the next guest. The entrance fee also covers a 30-minute video and a visit to the "catslide" house, built in 1700 and named for its steep roof. Tobacco grows in a neighboring plot. There is also a picnic table and a well of fresh water for filling water bottles.

After your visit, return to Chapel Point Road and turn left.

5.2 **Turn left onto MD 6.**

At the intersection with MD 6 stands Murphy's (left), a store offering liquor and groceries. You can sit at picnic tables outside and order barbecued ribs cooked in a pit on the grounds.

5.5 **Turn right onto Rose Hill Road, which climbs a steep hill.**

6.2 **Take a left onto the dirt road (driveway) to Habre de Venture, the Thomas Stone National Historic Site. It's open Wednesday through Sunday 9–5.**

Built by Thomas Stone, a signer of the Declaration of Independence, the house is strange, almost unique. Its hip-roofed central building and two wings form a crescent. Stone is buried on the grounds—you can see his grave from the dirt road that leads to the house.

After your visit, reverse direction, backtracking down Rose Hill Road.

6.9 **Turn left onto MD 6.**

7.2 **Turn right onto Chapel Point Road.**

12.3 **Follow Chapel Point Road around a sharp, uphill curve.**

12.4 **Return to St. Ignatius.**

Bicycle Repair Service

Mike's Bikes of Waldorf, 2102 Crain Highway, Waldorf, Maryland (301-870-6600)

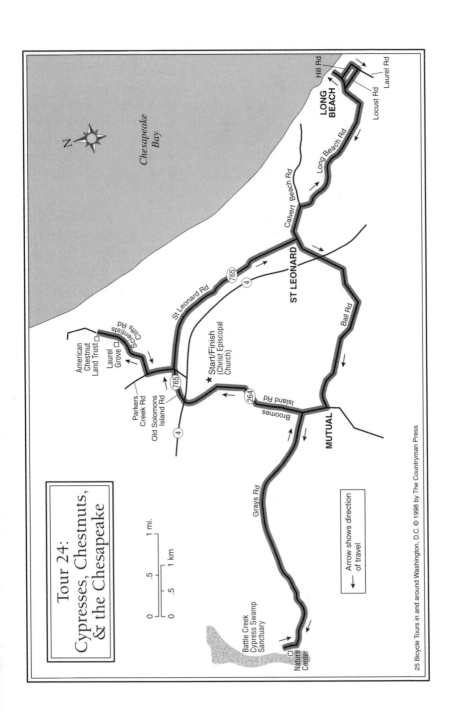

Tour 24:
Cypresses, Chestnuts,
& the Chesapeake

Chesapeake Bay

N

LONG BEACH

Hill Rd
Laurel Rd
Locust Rd

Long Beach Rd

Calvert Beach Rd

765

4

St Leonard Rd

ST LEONARD

Ball Rd

Scientists Cliffs Rd

American Chestnut Land Trust
Laurel Grove

765

Parkers Creek Rd
Old Solomons Island Rd

4

★ Start/Finish (Christ Episcopal Church)

264

Brooms Island Rd

MUTUAL

Grays Rd

Battle Creek Cypress Swamp Sanctuary
Nature Center

1 mi.
.5
1 km
.5
0
0

← Arrow shows direction of travel

25 Bicycle Tours in and around Washington, D.C. © 1998 by The Countryman Press

24

Cypresses, Chestnuts, and the Chesapeake

Location: *Calvert County, Maryland*
Terrain: *Moderately hilly*
Road conditions: *Paved roads, a few stretches with moderately heavy traffic*
Distance: *24.1 miles*
Highlights: *The American Chestnut Land Trust, Long Beach, the Battle Creek Cypress Swamp and Nature Center, Christ Episcopal Church*

Calvert County, Maryland, is a finger of land between the Chesapeake Bay and the Patuxent River just south of Washington. Its main highway, MD 4, is a southern extension of Washington's Pennsylvania Avenue. Although suburbia is creeping inexorably southward through Calvert, it's still a county where time is marked by the rhythm of the tobacco-growing, oystering, and crabbing seasons.

This tour visits a bayside community and also takes in two of the county's more unusual attractions: the American Chestnut Land Trust, where dedicated volunteers are trying to revive the blighted and almost extinct American chestnut and where one 80-foot specimen still stands tall; and the Battle Creek Cypress Swamp, a sanctuary for the northernmost stand of the bald cypress.

The trip begins at Christ Episcopal Church in Port Republic. The church, whose present building dates from 1772, is locally famous for the jousting tournament held on the grounds each August. (Jousting is the state sport of Maryland.) To reach the church parking lot from the Washington Beltway, take MD 4 south to the intersection with MD 264 (Broomes Island Road). Turn right onto MD 264 and continue 0.3 mile to the church (left). It's about an hour's drive from Washington.

0.0 Leave the Christ Church parking lot and turn right onto MD 264.

0.3 Cross MD 4 very carefully and continue on Old Solomons Island Road (MD 765), which is sometimes marked as St. Leonard Road.

0.8 At the intersection of Parkers Creek Road there's an antiques store. Turn left onto Parkers Creek Road.

1.1 Turn right onto Scientists Cliffs Road.

On your left on this rolling, wooded road is the Jewell Glass Laurel Grove. Dr. Jewell Glass, a mineralogist with the US Geological Survey, died in 1965 and willed this piece of land—steeply sloping and dominated by laurel thickets—to The Nature Conservancy.

2.0 On the left is the main entrance to the American Chestnut Land Trust.

Here dedicated volunteers—many of them scientists and residents of Scientists Cliffs—are trying to revitalize the American chestnut by breeding it with other strains of chestnut. Lock your bike and follow the hiking trail to one sturdy survivor, an 80-foot chestnut, blighted but unbowed. Take a trail map from the box in the small parking lot.

After your hike, return to the intersection with Parkers Creek Road.

2.9 Turn left onto Parkers Creek Road.

3.2 Turn left onto St. Leonard Road (MD 765 or Solomons Island Road).

This used to be the main road, before a modern MD 4 was completed a few years ago, so it's sort of a ghost highway, with services and businesses that have been bypassed by progress. It's a good biking road with a wide shoulder, and heavy traffic uses MD 4.

7.2 A cluster of buildings on your right marks the small settlement of St. Leonard.

Beuhler's Market is highly recommended for picnic supplies and carryout food. The crabcake and shrimp dinners, with freshly made fries, are especially good.

5.6 *At St. Leonard, turn left onto Calvert Beach Road.*

6.1 *Turn right onto Long Beach Road.*

8.2 *Long Beach Road ends at the beach in the old bungalow colony of Long Beach.*

Here houses built in the 1920s and 1930s nestle in the hills that overlook the water. After a picnic or walk on the beach, turn back onto Long Beach Road.

8.4 *Turn left onto Hill Road, which lives up to its name but affords a tour of this pleasant old resort town.*

9.0 *Hill Road ends. Turn right onto Laurel Road and take the next right turn onto Locust Road.*

9.4 *Turn left onto Long Beach Road.*

11.5 *Turn left onto Calvert Beach Road and continue back through St. Leonard and across MD 4, where Calvert Beach Road becomes Ball Road.*

Ball Road climbs some hills and skirts the rural settlement of Mutual.

14.4 *Ball Road ends. Turn right onto MD 264 (Broomes Island Road).*

14.6 *Turn left onto Grays Road.*

18.8 *Turn left into the driveway of the Battle Creek Cypress Swamp Sanctuary.*

The sanctuary and nature center are open April through September, Tuesday through Saturday 10–5 and Sunday 1–5. During the winter months, the area closes at 4:30. Admission is free.

The focal point of the preserve is a nature trail built on a boardwalk over the swamp. The majestic bald cypresses tower as high as a hundred feet overhead and their feathery deciduous needles form a cathedral-like canopy, sheltering many kinds of birds and splashing filtered light on the swamp below. Watch for turtles and frogs among the sleek knobs that poke through the mud. These knobs are the knees of the trees, an extension of the bald cypress root system. They help brace the trees and may provide oxygen to underwater roots. This really is a special place that, in the words of the promotional brochure, "recalls a time some

100,000 years ago when large parts of Maryland were covered with swamps, and saber-toothed tigers and mammoths roamed the landscape."

After your visit, turn right out of the parking lot onto Grays Road, heading back toward MD 264.

23.0 Grays Road ends. Turn left onto MD 264 (Broomes Island Road).

24.1 Turn right into Christ Church parking lot.

Bicycle Repair Service

Mike's Bikes of Waldorf, 2102 Crain Highway, Waldorf, Maryland (301-870-6600)

25
Covering the Bridges

Location: Frederick County, Maryland
Terrain: Moderately hilly
Road conditions: Paved country roads with little traffic
Distance: 24.6 miles
Highlights: Three covered bridges, Apple's Church, Catoctin Furnace, the
  Cozy Inn

Covered bridges make perfect sense: Since bridge surfaces freeze before solid highways, why not put a roof over them? But modern road planners don't like covered bridges, and the wooden structures, prey to the debilitating effects of time and weather as well as to modernization, are fast disappearing. There were once 52 covered bridges in Maryland. Only eight remain, and three of them are within easy cycling distance of the pleasant town of Thurmont, north of Frederick. All three bridges look exactly alike, constructed of red, beveled German clapboard. But getting to them takes you through pretty farm country where you'll find lots of cows, horses, and pigs to commune with. There are also picturesque towns and inviting streams. The Catoctin Mountains form a dramatic backdrop for the scenery, and you can enjoy them without having to climb them.

The tour begins in the parking lot of the Cozy Inn in Thurmont. To get there, take I-270 north from the Beltway to Frederick. At Frederick, I-270 runs into US 15. Take US 15 north to the Thurmont exit and follow the signs to the Cozy Inn. Tell the reservations clerk you'll be back in about four hours, and be sure to come back hungry. The all-you-can-eat buffet is not for the faint of heart.

0.0 Exit the parking lot and turn left onto Frederick Road.

0.3 Just past the community park, turn left onto Church Street.

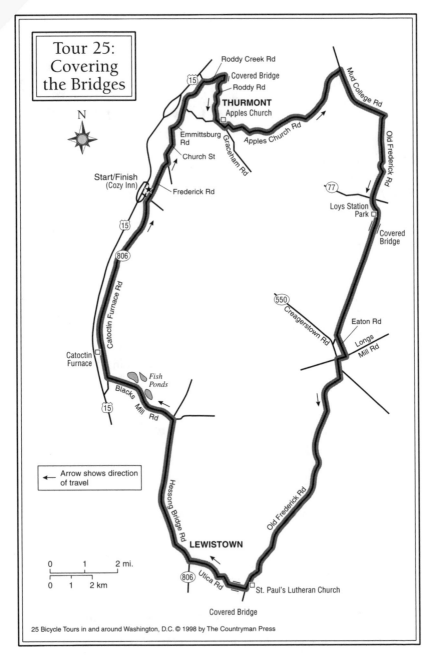

**Tour 25:
Covering
the Bridges**

N

Roddy Creek Rd

⬡15

Covered Bridge
Roddy Rd
THURMONT
Apples Church

Mud College Rd

Emmittsburg
Rd

Church St

Apples Church Rd

Graceham Rd

Old Frederick Rd

Start/Finish
(Cozy Inn)

Frederick Rd

⬡77

Loys Station
Park

⬡15

Covered
Bridge

⬡806

⬡550

Creagerstown Rd

Catoctin Furnace Rd

Eaton Rd

Longs
Mill Rd

Catoctin
Furnace

*Fish
Ponds*

Blacks
Mill Rd

⬡15

Old Frederick Rd

← Arrow shows direction
of travel

Hessong Bridge Rd

LEWISTOWN

0   1   2 mi.

0   1   2 km

⬡806
Utica Rd

St. Paul's Lutheran Church

Covered Bridge

25 Bicycle Tours in and around Washington, D.C. © 1998 by The Countryman Press

You are now in the heart of Thurmont, founded in 1751 by a westward-bound family who stopped here with a sick child. They stayed on, started a forge, and other industries grew up to serve the surrounding farms.

0.9 *Turn right onto Emmitsburg Road (MD 806), which passes a horse farm and then travels through a small industrial area.*

1.9 *Turn right onto Roddy Creek Road, which follows Owens Creek through a pleasant wooded area.*

2.4 *The first and smallest of the three covered bridges, a picturesque barn red, carries you over Owens Creek.*

This is a good spot for wading, and the horses in the neighboring field will probably come up to the fence to pose for pictures.

2.4 *After crossing the creek, make a sharp right onto Roddy Road, which takes you over rolling hills and past small farms.*

3.2 *At the intersection with Graceham Road, bear left. Then make the next left onto Apples Church Road.*

The stone church (left) that gives the road its name dates from 1826 and was built to serve the German community.

6.1 *Make a sharp right onto Mud College Road.*

This is a rural road that winds around to the left and has a short gravel stretch.

7.4 *Turn right onto Old Frederick Road.*

9.1 *At Loys Station Park, Old Frederick Road bears right, taking you over the second covered bridge.*

This bridge is also made of red, beveled German clapboard and also crosses Owens Creek. There's a swimming hole under the bridge, and just downstream the creek flows over some mini-rapids. This is an ideal picnic spot, with picnic tables but no changing facilities other than a portable toilet. After the park, Old Frederick Road climbs a hill. At the top you'll see a spectacular view of the Catoctins. A little farther on there's duck pond.

11.2 *Turn left onto Eaton Road.*

11.6 *Turn right onto Longs Mill Road and proceed to the intersection with Creagerstown Road (MD 550). Turn left.*

There's a small food store just after the intersection.

11.9 *Turn right onto Old Frederick Road, which cuts across some suburban developments.*

16.1 *St. Paul's Lutheran Church is on a hill to your left. Just past the church, turn right onto Utica Road.*

16.4 *Another red covered bridge carries Utica Road over Fishing Creek.*

The road then winds uphill and down.

17.1 *Utica Road ends. Turn right onto Hessong Bridge Road.*

18.1 *Martin's Grocery, in the village of Lewistown, is on your left.*

20.0 *Turn left onto Blacks Mill Road, which skirts Little Hunting Creek.*

The stream, which invites wading, is on your left. On your right are fish hatchery ponds, but there is no access to them from this road.

21.3 *Turn right onto Catoctin Furnace Road (MD 806).*

21.8 *The ruins on your left are the remains of Catoctin Furnace, which goes back to 1774.*

The shells used by the Continental Army at the battle of Yorktown were made here. The surrounding park has picnic tables. After you pass the furnace, Catoctin Furnace Road veers close to US 15, becoming a frontage road.

23.6 *The Blue Mountain Inn (right) is locally famous for its crabs.*

After passing the inn, the road descends on Thurmont, running a gamut of fast-food restaurants. Watch for traffic where Catoctin Furnace Road joins Frederick Road.

24.6 *Turn left into the Cozy Inn.*

Bicycle Repair Service

Frederick Bicycles, 1216 West Patrick Street, Frederick, Maryland (301-663-4452)

26
Over the River and through the Hills to Harpers Ferry

Location: *Maryland, Virginia, and West Virginia*
Metro access: *Alternate start at Dunn Loring*
Terrain: *A few steep hills in and on the approach to Harpers Ferry; otherwise rolling or flat*
Road conditions: *Two short stretches on heavily traveled highways with wide shoulders; a paved dedicated bike trail; lightly traveled country roads; an unpaved bike trail*
Distance: *54 miles*
Highlights: *A ride on the Jubal A. Early, historic Leesburg, the Washington and Old Dominion Trail, the Breaux Vineyards, the preserved Civil War–era town of Harpers Ferry, the Chesapeake and Ohio Canal*

Some say that the Civil War started not at Fort Sumter but at Harpers Ferry, where a fiery abolitionist named John Brown staged a daring raid on the federal arsenal in 1859. (Ironically, the first casualty of the raid was a free black man, commemorated in a memorial erected by the Daughters of the Confederacy.) The raiders were routed by federal troops under the command of Lt. Col. Robert E. Lee. Brown was hanged, but his song went marching on and became a rallying cry for the North.

Harpers Ferry's Lower Town, where this and more took place, is now a National Historical Park with an excellent interpretive program by the National Park Service. Getting there, of course, is more than half the fun of this trip, which begins with a ride on a ferryboat named after another Civil War character, Confederate Gen. Jubal Early. After passing through the beautiful Virginia courthouse town of Leesburg, the trip continues on a rails-to-trails byway, which ends at Purcellville, an antiques mecca.

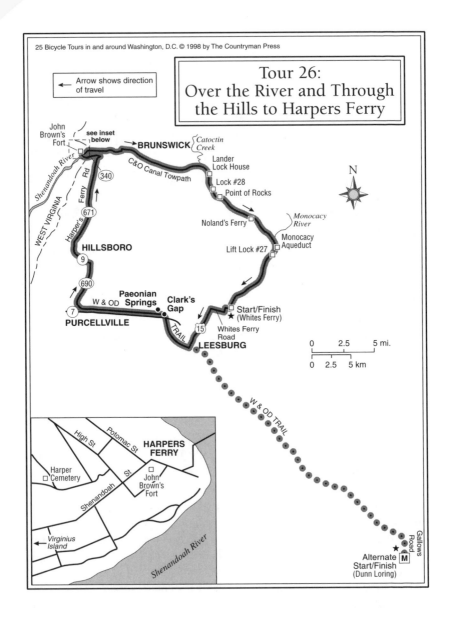

25 Bicycle Tours in and around Washington, D.C. © 1998 by The Countryman Press

Arrow shows direction
of travel

**Tour 26:
Over the River and Through
the Hills to Harpers Ferry**

John
Brown's
Fort

**see inset
below**

➤ **BRUNSWICK** *Catoctin
Creek*

Lander
Lock House

Shenandoah River

C&O Canal Towpath

(340)

Lock #28

Point of Rocks

N

WEST VIRGINIA

Harper's Ferry Rd

(671)

Noland's Ferry

*Monocacy
River*

HILLSBORO

9

Monocacy
Aqueduct

Lift Lock #27

(690)

**Paeonian
Springs**

W & OD

**Clark's
Gap**

Start/Finish
★ (Whites Ferry)

7

PURCELLVILLE

TRAIL

(15)

Whites Ferry
Road

LEESBURG

0   2.5   5 mi.

0   2.5   5 km

W & OD TRAIL

High St

Potomac St

**HARPERS
FERRY**

Harper
Cemetery

St

John
Brown's
Fort

Gallows Road

Shenandoah

★

Alternate M
Start/Finish
(Dunn Loring)

*Virginius
Island*

Shenandoah River

Country roads lead between the hills and down to Harpers Ferry, at the confluence of the Potomac and Shenandoah Rivers. After a respite in one of the town's charming bed & breakfast inns, the return trip crosses the Potomac on a railroad trestle and follows the Chesapeake and Ohio Canal towpath back to Whites Ferry.

To reach Whites Ferry from the Beltway, take I-270 north to the MD 28 exit and head west to the intersection of MD 107, Whites Ferry Road. Turn left onto Whites Ferry Road and follow it to the end. There is a large parking lot and a store for stocking up on picnic supplies. The ferry runs seven days a week, year-round, beginning about 6 AM and running till 11 PM except in winter, when it stops at 8 PM. During unusually high water on the Potomac, the ferry may not operate. Call 301-349-5200.

The sole survivor of about a hundred ferries operating on the Potomac, Whites Ferry has been in business for about 150 years. Gen. Jubal Early crossed the river hereabouts on his way to raid Washington in 1864, and recrossed shortly thereafter when the raid failed. The boat that is his namesake glides across the Potomac on a cable, and cyclists pay only a small fee.

Note: If you would like a Metro start for this tour, the most convenient one is Dunn Loring, which is 0.7 mile from the W&OD Trail via an on-sidewalk trail. Turn left onto the W&OD Trail and head west. At Leesburg, you will join the main tour. For the return trip, cross the Potomac on the Jubal A. Early and follow the directions to the W&OD Trail at the beginning of the main tour. Turn left onto the W&OD Trail and head east. At Gallows Road, turn right and return to the Dunn Loring Metro station. This will make a round trip of 102.6 miles.

Day 1

0.0 Ride off the ferry onto the Virginia side and follow the feeder road up a hill, through woods and rolling farmland to the junction with US 15.

1.2 Turn left onto US 15, riding on the shoulder.

3.2 Keep to your right when the road divides, following US 15 Business rather than Bypass.

Near this point, look for a historic marker commemorating the Civil War Battle of Ball's Bluff, a bloody skirmish that took place in

The *General Jubal A. Early,* a cable ferry, carries cyclists across the Potomac near the point where the boat's namesake crossed in 1864 after raiding Washington.

1861. Union troops were ferried across the canal on barges and many drowned when a boat capsized during the retreat. You are now entering Leesburg, named in honor of Francis Lightfoot Lee, a signer of the Declaration of Independence. US 15 becomes King Street, and is lined with shops and restaurants.

4.4 Turn right onto the W&OD Trail.

The trail follows the old roadbed of the Washington and Old Dominion Railroad, whose trains ran from 1859 to 1968. Passengers affectionately called the line "the Virginia Creeper." In 1982, the 45-mile right-of-way was acquired by the Northern Virginia Regional Park Authority and the paved trail was completed in 1988. It is used by walkers, joggers, in-line skaters, and equestrians as well as cyclists. Watch for horse piles. The trail soon leaves the backyards of Leesburg and wanders through countryside.

8.6 You have now climbed to the highest point on the trail, Clarks Gap. Pass under a hundred-year-old stone arch and cross over VA 7, following the trail signs across the bridge.

9.3 The trail passes through Paeonian Springs, a lovely town that includes the Museum of the American Workhorse.

11.3 The defunct Hamilton Railroad Station stands on your right. Washingtonians escaping the summer heat once disembarked here to cool off in the boardinghouses of this pre–Civil War Quaker settlement.

13.3 The trail seems to end here, but actually it turns left, crosses the VA 7 bypass, and leads into Purcellville. Follow the trail signs.

14.8 The trail ends at the old Purcellville Railroad Station.

Efforts are underway to turn the station into an end-of-trail facility with showers, rest rooms, and other amenities. Meanwhile, the town of Purcellville, to your left, offers antiques shops, food stores, and restaurants. Fran's Place, on Main Street, has hearty fare, including excellent milkshakes.

To continue to Harpers Ferry, turn right onto VA 690, which leads out of town and crosses the VA 7 bypass on a bridge.

The road continues through rolling farmland, with spectacular mountain views on your left.

Robert Harper, who started a ferry service near the confluence
of the Potomac and Shenandoah rivers in the mid 1700s,
also founded the town cemetery.

19.8 At the intersection with VA 9, turn left and follow the road through Hillsboro, whose antebellum stone houses line the road. The market at the Exxon station (left) stocks sandwiches and coffee.

21.8 On your left is Lynfield Farm, a picture-book, white-fenced horse farm.

22.4 At the intersection near a small store, turn right onto VA 671, Harpers Ferry Road.

This road cuts through the hills, with mountain views on both sides and cattle grazing in the foothills.

23.5 Breaux Vineyards (right) is open for tours on weekends.

26.2 St. Paul's Lutheran Church (left), a stone building dating from 1835, has an inviting graveyard.

30.0 After climbing a hill and enjoying a long descent to the river, turn left onto US 340, which has a wide shoulder affording good views of the boulder-strewn Potomac and the gorges on the Maryland side. Follow the bridge across the Shenandoah River into West Virginia.

32.0 Take a sharp right onto Shenandoah Street, the entrance to the lower town area of the historic district.

You will pass Virginius Island, the ruins of a once thriving industrial town drawing power from the Shenandoah River. The street leads directly into the preserved town, where you will find an excellent bookstore and information kiosk. Ask about ranger-led tours.

32.1 At the intersection of Shenandoah and Potomac Streets stands John Brown's Fort, actually the armory fire engine house, where he was captured 36 hours after his raid began.

Lock your bike hereabouts and double back one block along Shenandoah Street to High Street. Go about one block up High Street and turn left onto the town's famous stone steps, which lead past a church used as a field hospital during the Civil War and up to Jefferson Rock. Jefferson is reputed to have stood on this rock and remarked that the view—of the confluence of the Potomac and Shenandoah Rivers—was "worth a voyage across the Altantic."

After making your own assessment, follow the path to Harper Cemetery, burial place of Robert Harper, who ran a ferry service here in the mid-1700s.

Most of the bed & breakfasts (see below), as well as the Hilltop House hotel, are up High Street, a steep climb.

Day 2

For the return trip, go past John Brown's Fort and walk your bike across the river on the old railroad trestle. When you carry it down the stairs on the Maryland side, you will be on the C&O Canal towpath.

32.5 Turn right onto the towpath.

The canal, completed in 1850 at a total cost of $11 million, helped transport flour, grain, building stone, whiskey, and coal between Cumberland, Maryland, and Georgetown. The mules that pulled the barges walked on this towpath, now a 184-mile hiker-biker trail that runs between the mainly dry canal and the Potomac under a canopy of trees. The trail is unpaved and can be muddy in wet weather. Call 301-739-4200 for trail conditions.

38.0 The towpath passes under the bridge that leads across the river to Virginia.

This bridge is a descendant of one burned by Confederates during the Civil War. The surrounding town, Brunswick, is a busy railroad center.

39.7 Cross Catoctin Creek on Catoctin Aqueduct, a three-arch stone crossing trussed by cables.

41.3 Lander Lock House was home for the tender of Lift Lock #29.

Its six-foot lift was the smallest on the canal.

44.1 Just past Lock #28, you'll see the town of Point of Rocks.

This is a good place to buy food and view the landmark Queen Anne–style railroad station.

46.0 Stop at Nolands Ferry picnic area.

Like many picnic areas along the towpath, it offers tables, grills, drinking pumps, and portable rest rooms.

48.4 *The trail crosses the Monocacy River on Monacacy Aqueduct, a 516-foot span consisting of seven arches.*

The structure was completed in 1833 and carried the canal across the Monocacy. Look upriver for a view of Sugarloaf Mountain. A pleasant park surrounds the area where the Monocacy runs into the Potomac. After crossing the aqueduct, the towpath curves to the right, following the Potomac.

49.1 *A footbridge leads to the lockhouse for Lift Lock #27.*

49.2 *An electric generating plant lies on your left.*

54.0 *MD 107 crosses the towpath. Turn right onto this road to the Whites Ferry parking lot.*

Bicycle Repair Service

Bicycle Outfitters, 19 Catoctin Circle NE, Leesburg, Virginia (703-777-6126)

Bed & Breakfasts

Ranson-Armory House, 690 Washington Street, Harpers Ferry, West Virginia (304-535-2142)

Hilltop House Hotel, 400 East Ridge Road, Harpers Ferry, West Virginia (304-535-2132)

Let Backcountry Guides Take You There

Our experienced backcountry authors will lead you to the finest trails, parks, and back roads in the following areas:

50 Hikes Series

50 Hikes in the Maine Mountains
50 Hikes in Southern and Coastal Maine
50 Hikes in Vermont
50 Hikes in the White Mountains
50 More Hikes in New Hampshire
50 Hikes in Connecticut
50 Hikes in Massachusetts
50 Hikes in the Hudson Valley
50 Hikes in the Adirondacks
50 Hikes in Central New York
50 Hikes in Western New York
50 Hikes in New Jersey
50 Hikes in Eastern Pennsylvania
50 Hikes in Central Pennsylvania
50 Hikes in Western Pennsylvania
50 Hikes in the Mountains of North
     Carolina
50 Hikes in Northern Virginia
50 Hikes in Ohio
50 Hikes in Michigan

Walks and Rambles Series

Walks and Rambles on Cape Cod and
     the Islands
Walks and Rambles in Rhode Island
More Walks and Rambles in Rhode
     Island
Walks and Rambles on the Delmarva
     Peninsula
Walks and Rambles in Southwestern
     Ohio
Walks and Rambles in Ohio's Western
     Reserve
Walks and Rambles in the Western
     Hudson Valley
Walks and Rambles on Long Island

25 Bicycle Tours Series

25 Bicycle Tours in Maine
30 Bicycle Tours in New Hampshire
25 Bicycle Tours in Vermont
25 Mountain Bike Tours in Vermont
25 Bicycle Tours on Cape Cod and the
     Islands
25 Mountain Bike Tours in
     Massachusetts
30 Bicycle Tours in New Jersey
25 Mountain Bike Tours in New Jersey
25 Bicycle Tours in the Adirondacks
30 Bicycle Tours in the Finger Lakes
     Region
25 Bicycle Tours in the Hudson Valley
25 Bicycle Tours in the Twin Cities and
     Southeastern Minnesota
30 Bicycle Tours in Wisconsin
25 Mountain Bike Tours in the
     Hudson Valley
25 Bicycle Tours in Ohio's
     Western Reserve
25 Bicycle Tours in Maryland
25 Bicycle Tours on Delmarva
25 Bicycle Tours in and around
     Washington, D.C.
25 Bicycle Tours in Coastal Georgia and
     the Carolina Low Country
25 Bicycle Tours in the Texas Hill
     Country and West Texas

We offer many more books on hiking, fly-fishing, travel, nature, and other subjects. Our books are available at bookstores and outdoor stores everywhere. For more information or a free catalog, please call 1-800-245-4151 or write to us at The Countryman Press, PO Box 748, Woodstock, Vermont 05091. You can find us on the web at www.countrymanpress.com